Sylvia Walby, Jude Towers, Susie Balderston,
Consuelo Corradi, Brian Francis,
Markku Heiskanen, Karin Helweg-Larsen,
Lut Mergaert, Philippa Olive, Emma Palmer,
Heidi Stöckl and Sofia Strid

THE CONCEPT AND MEASUREMENT OF VIOLENCE AGAINST WOMEN AND MEN

D1643065

POLICY PRESS  POLICY & PRACTICE

First published in Great Britain in 2017 by

Policy Press
University of Bristol
1-9 Old Park Hill
Bristol
BS2 8BB
UK
+44 (0)117 954 5940
pp-info@bristol.ac.uk
www.policypress.co.uk

North America office:
Policy Press
c/o The University of Chicago Press
1427 East 60th Street
Chicago, IL 60637, USA
t: +1 773 702 7700
f: +1 773 702 9756
sales@press.uchicago.edu
www.press.uchicago.edu

British Library Cataloguing in Publication Data
A catalogue record for this book is available from the British Library.

Library of Congress Cataloging-in-Publication Data
A catalog record for this book has been requested.

ISBN 978-1-4473-3263-3 (paperback)
ISBN 978-1-4473-3265-7 (ePub)
ISBN 978-1-4473-3267-1 (Mobi)
ISBN 978-1-4473-3264-0 (ePdf)

The rights of Sylvia Walby, Jude Towers, Susie Balderston, Consuelo Corradi, Brian Francis, Markku Heiskanen, Karin Helweg-Larsen, Lut Mergaert, Philippa Olive, Emma Palmer, Heidi Stöckl and Sofia Strid to be identified as the authors of this work has been asserted by them in accordance with the Copyright, Designs and Patents Act 1988.

The statements and opinions contained within this publication are solely those of the author and not of the University of Bristol or Policy Press. The University of Bristol and Policy Press disclaim responsibility for any injury to persons or property resulting from any material published in this publication.

Policy Press works to counter discrimination on grounds of gender, race, disability, age and sexuality.

Cover design by Policy Press
Front cover: image kindly supplied by www.alamy.com

Contents

Glossary

ACE	Adverse Childhood Experiences
ACUNS	Academic Council of the United Nations
CAHRV	Coordinated Action on Human Rights Violations
CASI	Computer Assisted Self-Interviewing
CAT	*Convention Against Torture*
CEDAW	*Convention on the Elimination of Discrimination against Women*
CIN	Child In Need
COST	Cooperation in Science and Technology
CRC	*Convention on the Rights of the Child*
CSEW	Crime Survey for England and Wales
CTS	Conflict Tactics Scale
CWASU	Child and Woman Abuse Studies Unit (London Metropolitan University)
DEVAW	*Declaration on the Elimination of Violence against Women*
DGs	Directorate-Generals
DHS	Demographic and Health Surveys
GBD	Global Burden of Disease
EACEA	Education, Audiovisual and Culture Executive Agency
ECHR	*European Convention of Human Rights*
ECPAT	End Child Prostitution, Child Pornography and Trafficking of Children for Sexual Purposes

ECtHR	European Court of Human Rights
EEOC	Equal Employment Opportunity Commission
EHRC	Equality and Human Rights Commission
EIGE	European Institute for Gender Equality
EU	European Union
EVAW	End Violence Against Women
FGM	Female Genital Mutilation
FRA	Fundamental Rights Agency
GREVIO	Group of Experts on Action against Violence against Women and Domestic Violence
HEUNI	European Institute for Crime Prevention and Control
HMIC	Her Majesty's Inspectorate of Constabulary
ICCPR	International Covenant on Civil and Political Rights
ICCS	International Classification of Crime for Statistical Purposes
ICD-10	International Statistical Classification of Diseases, 10th revision
ICECI	International Classification of External Causes of Injury
ICESCR	*International Convention on Economic, Social and Cultural Rights*
ICTR	International Criminal Tribunal for Rwanda
ICTY	International Criminal Tribunal on Yugoslavia
IPFM	intimate partner or family member
ISG	Injury Surveillance Guidelines
ISHMT	International Shortlist for Hospital Morbidity Tabulation
IVAWS	International Violence against Women Survey
LGBQTI	lesbian, gay, bisexual, queer, transgender and intersex
NGO	non-governmental organisation
ONS	Office for National Statistics
PACE	Parents Against Child Sexual Exploitation

PI	Principal Investigator
SARC	Sexual Assault Referral Centre
SCCI	Standardisation Committee for Care Information
SDGs	Sustainable Development Goals
UN Women	UN Entity on Gender Equality and the Empowerment of Women
UN–CTS	United Nations Surveys on Crime Trends and the Operations of Criminal Justice Systems
UNESCO	*United Nations Educational, Scientific and Cultural Organization*
UNICEF	United Nations Children's Fund
UNODC	United Nations Office on Drugs and Crime
VAW	Violence Against Women
WAVE	Women Against Violence Europe
WHO	World Health Organization

Notes on authors

Sylvia Walby is Distinguished Professor of Sociology, UNESCO Chair of Gender Research and Director of the Violence and Society UNESCO Centre, Lancaster University, UK. She is a Fellow of the Academy of Social Sciences, UK. She is author – with Philippa Olive, Jude Towers, Brian Francis, Sofia Strid, Andrea Krizsán, Emanuela Lombardo, Corinne May-Chahal, Suzanne Franzway, David Sugarman, Bina Agarwal and Jo Armstrong – of *Stopping Rape: Towards a Comprehensive Policy* (Policy Press, 2015). She is also author of *Crisis* (Polity, 2015), *The Future of Feminism* (Polity, 2011) and *Globalization and Inequalities: Complexity and Contested Modernities* (Sage, 2009). Her current research focuses on trafficking in human beings and theorising violence.

Jude Towers is a doctor of applied social statistics, Lecturer in Sociology and Quantitative Methods, Associate Director of the Violence and Society UNESCO Centre and acting lead for the N8 Policing Research Partnership Training and Learning strand, Lancaster University, UK. She holds Graduate Statistician status from the Royal Statistical Society. She is author – with Sylvia Walby and Brian Francis – of 'Mainstreaming domestic and gender-based violence into sociology and the criminology of violence' (*Sociological Review*, 2014, 62: 187–214) and 'Is violent crime increasing or decreasing? A new methodology to measure repeat victimisation making visible the significance of gender and domestic relations' (*British Journal of Criminology*, 2015, 56(6) 1203-1234). Her current research focuses on the measurement of different forms of violence.

Susie Balderston is Research Fellow and Associate of the Violence and Society UNESCO Centre at Lancaster University, UK, Lecturer in Social Policy at Salford University, UK and Policy Director of Vision Sense (a user-led organisation of disabled people), UK. She served as Expert Advisor to the Equality and Human Rights Commission's 'Statutory inquiry into disability harassment' and 'Access to specialised victim support service for women with disabilities who have experienced violence' projects. She designs, mentors and evaluates user-led and service user involvement for disabled people and mental health survivor projects in social care, health and criminal justice.

Consuelo Corradi is Professor of Sociology and Vice-Rector at Lumsa University, Rome, Italy and Vice-Chair of the European Union (EU) Cooperation in Science and Technology (COST) Action IS 1206, 'Femicide across Europe'. Since 2016, she has been a visiting researcher at Cics Nova-Interdisciplinary Research Center for Social Sciences, Universidade Nova de Lisboa, Portugal. She was Vice-President of the European Sociological Association from 2007 to 2011. Since 2002, she has directed and codirected interdisciplinary research projects funded by the European Commission (EC) under the Daphne III, Joint Actions, Socrates–Grundtvig and Leonardo da Vinci frameworks. Her current research focuses on violence, cross-national comparison of policies on violence against women (VAW), femicide and theories of modernity.

Brian Francis is Professor of Social Statistics and Associate Director of the Violence and Society UNESCO Centre, Lancaster University, UK. He is a chartered statistician and quantitative criminologist with over thirty years of experience of statistical consultancy and applied statistical research. His recent criminological work has focused on the analysis of criminal careers and issues relating to serious crime, including homicide, kidnap, domestic violence and sex offending, as well as organised crime. His 230 publications span statistics, criminology, health, sociology, psychology and developing analytic approaches to quantitative data. His recent work includes papers on football and domestic violence, the desistance of sex offenders and the statistical modelling of terrorist networks.

Markku Heiskanen is Senior Researcher at the European Institute for Crime Prevention and Control, affiliated with the United Nations (HEUNI). He holds a PhD in Sociology from the University of Helsinki, Finland. He is an expert on comparative survey research, survey methodology, victim surveys, research on violence against women and quantitative crime analysis and has been involved in several victimisation survey projects, as well as studies on the costs of VAW. He has expertise in analysing United Nations Office on Drugs and Crime (UNODC) data and has participated in the work of the European Sourcebook Group, analysing crime trends in European countries.

Karin Helweg-Larsen is Emeritus Professor of Social Medicine and of Forensic Medicine at the University of Copenhagen, Denmark; Chair of the Nordic Research Network on VAW under the Nordic Council and of the Danish Research Network on Adverse Childhood Experiences (ACE); consultant at the World Health Organization (WHO) on gender based violence, Temporary Chair of the European Council's Working Group on violence against women and member of the Danish Observatory on VAW. She has published a number of articles on gender perspectives of human rights violations, the health consequences of violence against women and the societal and individual costs of violence.

Lut Mergaert is Doctor of Management Sciences and Research Director at Yellow Window, Antwerp, Belgium. Her work focuses on decision support studies for the public sector. She has been the Principal Investigator (PI) of many pan-European research projects on gender equality issues. Relevant publications include *Female Genital Mutilation in the European Union and Croatia* (Vilnius: European Institute for Gender Equality (EIGE), 2013), *Good Practices in Combating Female Genital Mutilation* (Vilnius: EIGE, 2013), *Estimation of Girls at Risk of Female Genital Mutilation in the European Union* (Vilnius: EIGE, 2015) and *Estimation of Girls at Risk of Female Genital Mutilation in the European Union: Step-by-Step Guide* (Vilnius: EIGE, 2015). She has also been the PI of the *Study on Gender-Based Violence in Sport* (EACEA/215/02EACEA/2015/02, 2016), funded by the Education, Audiovisual and Culture Executive Agency (EACEA) on behalf of the EC.

Philippa Olive is Senior Research Fellow in Health Services Research, University of Central Lancashire, UK. Philippa is a health and social scientist and multiple methodologist. Her research and scholarship have a number of strands, including gender-based violence, social determinants of health and complex public health concerns, health inequalities and applied health services research. Her research has explored the construction and classification of forms of gender-based violence during health consultations and in health information systems. Her work has investigated data categories and collection methods for forms of gender-based violence in health consultations, health records and national and international administrative health data systems, including the UK's National Health Service (NHS) datasets and the WHO's ICD–10. Philippa has expertise in methodologies for measuring the harms and impacts of gender-based violence and for estimating their economic cost.

Emma Palmer is Lecturer in Social Work, Associate of the Centre for Child and Family Justice and Associate of the Violence and Society UNESCO Centre at Lancaster University, UK. She is a Registered Social Worker in England and prior to academia worked in child and families services. She then developed expertise in child trafficking and spent two years at ECPAT UK in a national training and development post. She coedited the first book on child trafficking in the UK, is author, with Sylvia Walby, Jude Towers, Brian Francis, Karen Shire, Liz Kelly, Birgit Apitzsch, Jo Armstrong, Susie Balderston, Adam

Fish, Claire Hardaker, Stuart Kirby, Corinne May-Chahal and Emma Palmer, of the EC-commissioned *Study on Comprehensive Policy Review of Anti-Trafficking Projects funded by the European Commission* (Brussels: European Commission, 2016) and has published academic articles in the field of child trafficking.

Heidi Stöckl is Lecturer in Global Health and Development, London School of Hygiene and Tropical Medicine, UK and Honorary Senior Lecturer at the University of Witwatersrand, South Africa. She is author – with Karen Devries, Alexander Rotstein, Naeemah Abrahams, Jaqueline Campbell, Charlotte Watts and Claudia-Garcia Moreno – of 'The global prevalence of intimate partner homicide: a systematic review' (*The Lancet*, 2013, 382: 859–65). She conducted the first prevalence study on intimate partner violence during pregnancy in Germany. Her current research focuses on prevalence, risk factors and health outcomes of intimate partner violence, intervention research, female and child homicide, human trafficking and labour exploitation.

Sofia Strid is Associate Professor of Gender Studies and Senior Lecturer in Political Science at Örebro University, Sweden and Co-Director of the GEXcel International Collegium for Advanced Transdisciplinary Gender Studies, Sweden. She is the editor of the *Nordic Journal for Gender Studies*. She is author – with Sylvia Walby (lead), Philippa Olive, Jude Towers, Brian Francis, Andrea Krizsán, Emanuela Lombardo, Corinne May-Chahal, Suzanne Franzway, David Sugarman, Bina Agarwal and Jo Armstrong – of *Stopping Rape: Towards a Comprehensive Policy* (Policy Press, 2015) and – with Lut Mergaert, Catarina Arnaut, Marja Exterkate and Siobahn O'Brien – of *Estimation of Girls at Risk of Female Genital Mutilation in the European Union* (Vilnius: European Institute for Gender Equality, 2015). Her current research focuses on violence regimes.

Acknowledgements

This publication builds on previous work funded by the Council of Europe: *Ensuring Data Collection and Research on Violence Against Women and Domestic Violence – Article 11 of the Istanbul Convention*, prepared by Sylvia Walby (Strasbourg: Council of Europe, 2016).

It draws on many years of research funded by multiple sources. We thank the following.

Sylvia Walby: Council of Europe; European Commission; European Parliament; European Institute for Gender Equality; UN Women; UN Economic Commission for Europe; UNESCO; UK Home Office; Women and Equality Unit; Equality and Human Rights Commission; Trust for London; Northern Rock Foundation; Economic and Social Research Council; Security Lancaster; and UK National Institute for Health Research.

Jude Towers: European Commission; European Parliament; Trust for London; Northern Rock Foundation; and the Economic and Social Research Council.

Susie Balderston: European Commission; EU Daphne III; Equality and Human Rights Commission; Healthwatch; Skills for Care; Annette Lawson Charitable Trust; Heritage Lottery Fund; UK Department of Health; and Northern Rock Foundation.

ACKNOWLEDGEMENTS

Consuelo Corradi: COST; Cooperation in Science and Technology; Italian Ministry of Research; EU Daphne III; and the Socrates-Grundvtig Program. The open-access license was co-funded by a publications grant from Lumsa University.

Brian Francis: European Commission; European Parliament; Economic and Social Research Council; and the Home Office.

Markku Heiskanen: Ministry of Health and Social Affairs/Council for Equality, Finland; Statistics Finland; European Institute for Gender Equality; European Union Agency for Fundamental Rights; European Commission; and Council of Europe.

Karin Helweg-Larsen: Y–SAV European Network; European Joint Research; EC Daphne; Danish Research Network on Child Sexual Abuse; Nordic Council for Criminal Prevention; EU Daphne; Danish Minister of Health; European Women's Health Network; Health Care in Europe; and NorVold Nordic Council.

Lut Mergaert: European Institute for Gender Equality; European Commission and Education; Audiovisual and Culture Executive Agency.

Philippa Olive: European Parliament; European Institute for Gender Equality; and UK National Institute for Health Research.

Emma Palmer: European Commission; and Parents Against Child Sexual Exploitation (PACE).

Heidi Stöckl: The Rhodes Scholarship; Medical Research Council; Economic and Social Research Council; World Health Organization; and the British Academy.

Sofia Strid: European Commission; European Institute for Gender Equality; European Parliament; Equality and Human Rights

Commission; EU Daphne III; Swedish Research Council and Örebro University.

Thanks also for very helpful comments on the project or draft manuscript to Jo Armstrong; Hilary Fisher; Liz Kelly; Rosa Logar; Carolina Lasen Diaz and Sogeti.

INTRODUCTION: MEASURING VIOLENCE TO END VIOLENCE

Violence matters. It wrecks lives. It causes injury and misery. Violence is both a cause and consequence of inequality. It is a violation of human rights. Violence is a detriment to health and to sustainable economic development.

Ending violence (or just reducing it) would be a major contribution to human wellbeing. A life free from violence is much valued. Preventing violence is a widely shared goal.

How? In order to end violence, a theory of change in violence is needed. In order to know what works to reduce violence, it is necessary to test theory with evidence. But even evidence as to whether the rate of violence is going up or down is hard to establish. This book seeks to improve the measurement of violence as a contribution towards zero violence.

Introduction

Lethal violence is enormous. There are nearly half a million (437,000) intentional homicides globally each year[1]

Lethal violence is gendered. Globally, 95% of perpetrators of intentional homicide are male. Every year, intimate partners or family members perpetrate nearly 64,000 intentional homicides; two thirds of victims are female. Half the intentional homicides of women are perpetrated by an intimate partner or other family members, compared to 6% of intentional homicides of men[2].

Violence against women is widespread. Globally, one in three women worldwide will experience physical or sexual violence in their lifetime; 30% of women who have been in an intimate relationship experience physical or sexual violence from their intimate partner[3]. In England and Wales, women were the victims in over half (52%) of violent crimes (violence against the person) recorded by the police in 2015[4]. Half of such violent crimes against women were domestic abuse-related, compared to 16% of those against men[5].

Violence against women has been increasing, while violence against men is still falling. In England and Wales between 2008/09 and 2013/14, the rate of violent crime against women increased significantly while the rate of violent crime against men decreased

---

[1] United Nations Office on Drugs and Crime (UNODC) (2013) *Global Study on Homicide*. Geneva, UNODC.

[2] UNODC (2013) *Op cit*. Footnote 1.

[3] World Health Organization (WHO) (2016) *Violence against Women: Intimate Partner and Sexual Violence against Women*. Fact sheet. www.who.int/mediacentre/factsheets/fs239/en/ [November 2016].

[4] In Sweden, 47% of violent crimes against the person, including gross violations of integrity, were against women in 2015 (Swedish National Council for Crime Prevention's [Brottsförebyggande Rådet (BRÅ)] Database on Reported Crime.)

[5] Office for National Statistics (ONS) (2016) *Focus on Violent Crime and Sexual Offences: Year Ending March 2015*. Cardiff, ONS.

significantly[6]. In England and Wales, there were over 88,000 sexual offences in 2014/15 – the highest figure recorded by the police since the introduction of the National Crime Recording Standard in 2002[7]. The harms from violence are unevenly distributed. Violence against women is a major cause and consequence of gender inequality. Yet, most official crime statistics render it invisible. Gender was not conceptualised as a significant category when these statistical systems were established. Attempt at reform has led to the establishment of a parallel universe of statistics that concerns women only, which means that gender is recognised, but segregated and marginalised. A dichotomy of 'no gender' or 'women only' has emerged.

The United Nations (UN) is an example of this dichotomy. The United Nations Office on Drugs and Crime (UNODC) makes gender invisible in its main categories for counting violent crime. The UN Entity on Gender Equality and the Empowerment of Women (UN Women) focuses on women only in its recommendations for statistics on violence. This dichotomy is found in many other places. In the European Union (EU), Eurostat uses a classification of violent crimes devoid of gender while the Fundamental Rights Agency conducts a survey on violence against women only. In the UK there is a slightly different dichotomy; headline statistics on violent crime make gender invisible while statistics on domestic abuse are separated from the main crime statistics. This state of affairs reflects divisions in the conceptualisation of violence and gender.

The way forward is to include gender within mainstream statistics and indicators. This requires official bodies to disaggregate their statistics by gender – not to treat gender as a secondary optional category

---

6   Walby, S., Towers, J. and Francis, B. (2016) 'Is the rate of violent crime increasing or decreasing? A new methodology to measure repeat attacks making visible the significance of gender and domestic relations', *British Journal of Criminology*, 56 (6): 1203–34. In Sweden, reported physical assault against women rose from 24,097 in 2005 to 31,262 in 2015, while falling for men in the same period from 40,262 to 39,245 (Swedish National Council for Crime Prevention's [Brottsförebyggande Rådet (BRÅ)] Database on Reported Crime. http://statistik. bra.se/solwebb/action/index [November 2016]).

7   ONS (2016) *Op cit.* Footnote 5.

or to collect data on women only. The mainstream framework also requires revision to include the forms of violence disproportionately experienced by women as well as those experienced by men.

This book offers a solution to the current choice between invisibility of gender and segregation of women in the measurement of violence. It offers new thinking on the concept of gender, drawing on developments in gender theory. Five 'gender saturated' dimensions are identified and defined so they can be measured. These enable the mainstreaming of gender in violence instead of the unsatisfactory alternatives currently in place.

What is violence?

The meaning of the concept 'violence' is contested. It has been stretched beyond physicality so that it encompasses many forms of power and harm, losing its distinctiveness, becoming submerged within notions of 'abuse' and 'coercion'. For the purposes of a theory of change – in order to potentially make visible the relationship between violence and other forms of power and to identify the levers of transformation – it is better to restrict the concept of 'violence' to a specific and precise definition connected to intended physical acts that cause harm. Yet, many of those who use a precise definition of violence underestimate the extent of violence against women, leaving this dimension invisible.

Contribution to the analysis of violence

Violence should be analysed as an institution in its own right. Violence is distinct from other forms of power and coercion. This book offers a route through the debates on violence to a consistent definition suitable for social scientists as well as practitioners. It provides a typology of forms of violence rooted in the principles of international law. The focus is on violence that is illegal and criminal rather than the legal and non-criminal violence of interstate war.

What is gender?

Gender relations are constituted in a social system. While the critical response to the traditional neglect of gender inequality often started with a focus on women, it has since developed into more subtle analyses of a range of dimensions of gender relations in social institutions. Some social institutions are more saturated by gender relations, more inflected or shaped by gender, than others.

Contribution to the analysis of gender

Gender relations are in part constituted through violence. Gender relations are part of the social relations that constitute the institution of violence. The analysis of the gendered nature of violence requires comparisons between women and men, which are not possible if the analytic focus and data collected concern women only. The development of the measurement of violence against women and men deepens the field of gender analysis.

What are statistics?

Statistics matter. Statistics entrench or contest existing social relations. Statistical systems embed concepts and definitions oriented towards theories and policy goals developed in previous eras. They should adapt if they are to be relevant to new policy goals and be informed by the current state of the art in social science. Today, the statistical categories that make gender-based violence near invisible in official policy are being challenged. In the case of violence, it is important to be able to know if violence is going up or down and if it is more or less common in one country or another.

Statistics summarise the world. An indicator is a statistic that acts as a meaningful summary of a mass of complicated data. It should be theoretically relevant, conceptually clear, practical in drawing on existing data and an easy-to-understand tool to assist decision-making by the public, policy makers and politicians. Statistics enable the testing of theory and the effectiveness of policy.

Contribution to statistics

This book offers a new measurement framework through which violence can be theorised, rather than just more data collection. This includes proposals that meet the call for indicators by the UN for its Sustainable Development Goals, the Council of Europe for its *Istanbul Convention on Preventing and Combating Violence against Women and Domestic Violence*, the EU for its strategy on violence against women and the UK Office for National Statistics for its reviews of domestic abuse and crime statistics.

This book reviews and consolidates new developments in theory and policy to produce a new measurement framework and indicators for violence against women and men relevant to the contemporary world. Mainstreaming gender into official statistics on violence, especially violent crime, is the purpose of this book. It makes proposals for the measurement of violence that draw on conceptual and theoretical debates. It is an intervention in contemporary policy debates relevant to policy makers. It is also a review and analysis of the processes of knowledge construction, relevant to students on social science courses from social policy to social statistics, sociology to politics, methodology to social theory.

The conclusions of the book derive from the 12 authors' decades of research and policy engagement in the field of gender-based violence.

Developing a theory of change

Why has violence fallen over centuries[8], only to start to rise again in recent years? Why do some countries (such as the US) have higher rates of violence than others (such as most of those in Europe)[9]? Why are

---

[8] Pinker, S. (2011) *The Better Angels of our Nature*. London, Allen Lane.
[9] Walby, S. (2009) *Globalisation and Inequalities*. London, Sage.

changes in the rates of violence different between women and men[10]? Explaining these variations requires a theory of change[11]. It requires the specification and testing of theories[12]. Are variations in violence explained by variations in inequality? Are both the cause (inequality) and consequence (variations in violence) gendered? Are the relevant inequalities economic, or are they political too? Are variations in violence explained by variations in self-control, or by the activities of the criminal justice system?

The purpose of developing a violence measurement framework is to contribute to ending violence by better constructing the knowledge base on which public debate, policy and politics draws. A coherent measurement framework and associated indicators would support the development of the theory of violence that would explain its variations. Identification and analysis of variations in gendered violence enable the testing of theories regarding causes of this violence and what might be effective in its prevention. Without robust evidence as to whether there is more or less gendered violence under some circumstances than others, it is hard to test theories regarding the causes of variations in this violence. There have been many attempts to build such theories that have been somewhat under-informed by evidence. The measurement framework and indicators will contribute to the collection of the robust evidence needed for theory development.

Only when violence is precisely delineated can its relationship with other forms of power and harm be properly investigated. Only if the distinctiveness of violence as a form of power – with distinctive modalities and rhythms of harm – is specified can the ways it links to other forms of power and harm be investigated. It is important to investigate the relationship between economic inequality and violence rather than to merge them into a single concept of financial abuse.

---

[10] Walby, S., Towers, J. and Francis, B. (2016) *Op cit.* Footnote 6.
[11] Vogel, I. (2012) *Review of the use of 'Theory of Change' in international development.* London, UK Department for International Development. https://assets.publishing.service.gov.uk/media/57a08a5ded915d3cfd00071a/DFID_ToC_Review_VogelV7.pdf [November 2016].
[12] Pawson, R. and Tilley, N. (1997) *Realistic Evaluation.* Thousand Oaks, Sage.

It is important to know whether gender stereotypes – such as in pornography – are significant in generating violence, rather than to declare that they are already also violence. It is important to know how gender intersects with other inequalities in the production of violence.

Establishing the concepts and definitions of 'violence' and 'gender' is necessary to develop theory and the measurement framework. The boundary between 'violence' and 'not violence' has been drawn in different places. For some, 'violence' is broadly defined as any major detriment or harm to human wellbeing; for others, 'violence' is more narrowly and precisely defined to include only those harms, intended by other people, which result from unwanted physical contact. Adjacent to this are different understandings of severity, repetition and duration. The concept of gender might initially appear to depend on a simple dichotomy, but the extent to which social systems, institutions and practices are saturated with gender is a subtler question. Gender is more than the distinction between male and female, as the significance of transgender indicates. Gender may be addressed by focusing on women, disaggregating data by gender in existing categories and mainstreaming gender into existing categories – both to make gender visible and to transform these categories. The process of theoretical development proposed here can be described as 'mainstreaming'. This involves mutual adjustments in both the 'specialised' perspective (here, 'violence against women and domestic violence') and the 'mainstream' perspective (including the criminal justice, health and employment systems).

The development of a theory of change depends on the investigation of the links between violence, gender and other aspects of social systems. At minimum, these other aspects include the significance of varying forms of criminal and civil legal justice, as well as health, welfare and specialised services and patterns of social, economic and political inequality.

Policy development

The measurement of violence is of particular relevance to the policy fields of crime, health, social and welfare services, human rights, security and gender equality. In Europe and the Global North, the most developed measurement practices concerning violence are those in the field of crime. The delineation of what counts as 'crime' is routinely subjected to democratic debate in parliaments, implemented in codes elaborated by civil servants and national statistical offices and analysed by academics. Violence is a central issue in international human rights legal instruments; its practical articulation is currently undergoing development[13]. Violence is increasingly identified as an issue of health[14], especially public health. Violence within a state has often been analytically separated from violence between states, though including both contexts can be helpful for analysis of changes in rates of violence[15].

The significance of the gender dimension of violence has been promoted by a multiplicity of feminist engagements[16]. These have identified the importance of violence against women for gender equality in a range of settings: from the home to the workplace, the street and conflict zones. Feminists have mobilised as grassroots

---

[13] United Nations (UN) (2015) *Sustainable Development Goals*. www.un.org/sustainabledevelopment/sustainable-development-goals/ [November 2016]; Council of Europe (2011) *Convention on Preventing and Combating Violence against Women and Domestic Violence (Istanbul Convention)*.

[14] Krug, E., Dahlberg, L., Mercy, J., Zwi, A. and Lozano, R. (eds) (2002) *World Report on Violence and Health*. Geneva, WHO; WHO (2014) *Global Status Report on Violence Prevention*. Geneva, WHO; WHO (2014) *Female Genital Mutilation*. Fact sheet no. 241. Geneva, WHO.

[15] Pinker, S. (2011) *Op cit*. Footnote 8; Walby, S. (2013) 'Violence and society: introduction to an emerging field of sociology', *Current Sociology*, 61(2): 95–111; Kaldor, M. (2006) *New and Old Wars*. 2nd ed. Cambridge, Polity Press.

[16] Dobash, R. E and Dobash, R. P. (1992) *Women, Violence and Social Change*. London, Routledge; Hague, G. and Malos, E. (1993) *Domestic Violence: Action for Change*. Cheltenham, New Clarion Press; Walby, S. (2011) *The Future of Feminism*. Cambridge, Polity Press; Weldon, S. L. and Htun, M. (2012), 'The civic origins of progressive policy change: combating violence against women in global perspective, 1975–2005', *American Political Science Review*, 106(3): 548–69.

movements and non-governmental civil society organisations, as well as developing specialised policy machineries within states. These projects to end violence against women have been local, national and international in scope. They are part of a wave of gender democratisation in which the gender gap in political decision-making has been reduced. This gender democratisation is one of the reasons behind the challenge to rethink the categories in which violence statistics are collected, so they can make visible its gender dimensions.

Measurement framework

This book offers a coherent and consistent 'measurement framework' rather than merely better practices for 'collecting data'. This framework enables data produced by one agency to be relevant for others and supports better theorisation of changes to the extent and form of violence.

There has been ambivalence towards, if not rejection of, quantitative methods in feminist research[17]. Qualitative methodology has sometimes been preferred on the grounds that it is closer to women's experience and hence their standpoint[18], though not all accept this position[19] and, in its purer forms, it has diminished over time[20]. This ambivalence draws on a wider distrust of the use of numbers in policy making[21], including the role of indicators in global governance[22]. But information in quantitative form is better understood as just another terrain of

[17]   Buss, D. (2015) 'Measurement imperatives and gender politics: an introduction', *Social Politics*, 22(3): 381–9.

[18]   Oakley, A. (1991) 'Interviewing women: a contradiction in terms', in Roberts, H. (ed.) *Doing Feminist Research*. London, Routledge and Kegan Paul: 30–61.

[19]   Scott, J. (2010) 'Quantitative methods and gender inequalities', *International Journal of Social Research Methodology*, 13(3): 223–36; Cohen, R. L., Hughes, C. and Lampard, R. (2011) 'The methodological impact of feminism: a troubling issue for sociology', *Sociology*, 45: 570–86.

[20]   Oakley, A. (1998) 'Gender, methodology and people's way of knowing: some problems with feminism and the paradigm debate', *Sociology*, 32: 707–32.

[21]   Porter, T. M. (1995) *Trust in Numbers*. Princeton, Princeton University Press.

[22]   Merry, S. E. (2011) 'Measuring the world: indicators, human rights, and global governance', *Current Anthropology*, 52: S83–S95.

argumentation[23]; just another modality of the truth regime. Scientific procedures, for all their weaknesses, contest as well as reproduce power[24]. Rather than stand aside, it is important to join the argument and contribute to the construction of the best measurement framework possible under the circumstances.

This involves finding a way through competing principles around which to cohere. The design of the framework affects the categories within which data is collected, thereby narrowing some avenues for understanding and action while widening others.

The data collected needs to be relevant and coordinated. This is best achieved when the categories in which data is collected are the same as the categories used by agencies working to protect victims and prevent violence. The categories used in the measurement framework should correspond to the categories in the conceptual framework within which public agencies' interventions are developed. This means that administrative and survey data should use the same definitions and the same units of measurement. This is not always current practice, since data collection has developed for specific purposes rather than as part of an integrated system designed to prevent violence. For example, agencies such as the police collect data relevant to the police, while academics conduct surveys using categories that are relevant to their theories. Cooperation between agencies is needed to build a framework that allows the collection of data relevant to the wider purpose of ending violence.

The development of a shared framework requires the identification of a coherent set of principles and of places where variations, between forms of violence and between policy fields, are sufficiently substantial to require accommodation. It is necessary to find an appropriate balance between coherence based on principles and variation based on real-world practicalities. The key set of principles underpinning the framework in this book is rooted in international law on violence; in

23   Johnson, H. (2015) 'Degendering violence', *Social Politics*, 22(3): 390–410.
24   Walby, S. (2001) 'Against epistemological chasms: the science question in feminism revisited', *Signs*, 26: 485–509.

particular, UN-led legal instruments. The practices that give effect to the principles require further development. There is less coherence in international law on gender than there is on violence. At least three approaches to gender can be discerned: universalism, which can lead to gender invisibility; a focus on women, in which violence is seen as a violation of women's human rights; and gender mainstreaming, in which violence is understood as a form of gender discrimination.

The measurement framework needs to address two essential dimensions of violence and of gender:

- *What is violence*: definition, thresholds and measures of seriousness, units of measurement and other technical and counting issues.
- *What is gender*: the sex of victim and perpetrator and further gender saturated dimensions, including the relationship between perpetrator and victim and whether there is a sexual aspect or a gendered motivation.

Indicators

Indicators are statistics that summarise complex quantitative information in a way that is meaningful to the public and policy makers[25]. They should have a direct and proportionate relationship with the 'real' phenomena they represent so that they are not misleading to those who are not 'experts'. The production of indicators for violence that are based on principles and viable in practice are discussed in Chapter Seven.

Identifying the relationship between the data and the 'real' rate of violence is not easy. Many proposed 'indicators' have an indeterminate relationship with the 'real' rate of violence. The relationship between the 'statistic', the 'concept' and the 'real world' is complex and evolving. An increase in the amount of violence made visible in administrative

---

[25] Berger-Schmitt, R. and Jankowitsch, B. (1999) *Systems of Social Indicators and Social Reporting*. EU Reporting Working Paper No. 1. Mannheim, Centre for Survey Research and Methodology.

or survey data has an uncertain relationship with the 'real' level of violence. There is an ever-present danger that elevating particular pieces of 'data' into 'indicators' of the real level of violence runs the risk of creating an inverse relationship between 'recorded violence' and 'real violence'. Ensuring no perverse effects is the biggest and most important challenge of all. This challenge is differently articulated depending on whether data is collected through administrative or survey instruments and further varies for different forms of violence, which vary in their ease and robustness of measurement. In particular, it is important that indicators that purport to measure changes in the 'real' rate of violence do not merely measure the recording of violence, since that would create a perverse incentive for policy bodies. It is important to ensure that the underpinning data is not open to manipulation and that there is no incentive to under-record in order to make it look as if the rate of violence is lower than it is in reality[26].

With the exception of homicide, the scale of violence recorded by all administrative data systems (criminal justice, health care and so on) is significantly lower than the 'real' rate of violence. Not only do these systems under-record the scale of violence; they also under-record it inconsistently. As such, the direction of change in the administrative data (for example, an increase in police-recorded crime) cannot be relied upon to indicate the direction of change in the real level of violence in the population. Thus, the data from which indicators are derived means the indicators themselves are contested. We offer solutions based on the latest scholarship.

[26]   Walby, S. (2007) *Indicators to Measure Violence against Women*. Report for UNDAW and UNECE for UN Expert meeting, Geneva, 8–10 October 2007; Walby, S. (2008) 'From statistics to indicators: how to convert information from surveys into practical indicators', in Aromaa, K. and Heiskanen, M. (eds) *Victimisation Surveys in Comparative Perspective*. Helsinki, Heuni: 180–8; Walby, S. and Armstrong, J. (2010) 'Measuring equality: data and indicators in Britain', *International Journal of Social Research Methodology*, 13: 237–49; Walby, S. and Armstrong, J. (2011) 'Developing indicators of fairness', *Social Policy & Society*, 10: 205–18.

Coordination

Achieving an effective measurement framework and populating it with reliable data require coordination. This necessitates reaching agreement on the categories, an authoritative process of quality assurance and developing institutionalised competence to sustain this over time and place.

Fully mobilising the potential of the data requires a research programme – to develop better data collection practices, to use the data to test theories of violence and to evaluate what works to reduce it.

Structure of the book

Following this introductory chapter, Chapter Two situates the recent calls for data, statistics and indicators in the context of the development of legal instruments and policies at international, regional and national levels.

Chapter Three situates discussion of the alternative approaches for the measurement framework in the context of developments in law, policy, scholarship and theory. It identifies the challenges in building a measurement framework for violence that is relevant to gender equality and offers solutions to them. It sets out the tensions between different theoretical and political perspectives, how these are articulated and how they can be addressed. For policy makers, this chapter will aid understanding as to why experts in the field disagree with each other. For students, this chapter will link the measurement debates with wider bodies of academic scholarship.

Chapter Four considers the extent to which the criteria in the framework need nuancing to capture the distinctions between different forms of violence. To address this question, it focuses on homicide; femicide; assault; domestic violence; rape; and FGM.

Chapter Five concerns practical aspects of measurement, as well as the necessity of understanding the substantive nature of violence in order to ensure technical aspects of measurement are appropriate, both in administrative data and surveys.

Chapter Six considers the institutions necessary to ensure meaningful, consistent and coherent data collection. Future research programmes are identified to improve and mobilise the data for developing theory and policy.

Concluding the book, Chapter Seven focuses on the proposed measurement framework for violence against women and men. It discusses indicators that enable identification of whether the rate of violence is increasing or decreasing and variations between women and men and between different countries. It also includes recommendations to national statistical institutes and other relevant entities.

LEGAL AND POLICY DEVELOPMENTS

Introduction

Policies to end violence need statistics that show whether violence is increasing or decreasing. Also important are statistics on variations in the rate and form of violence in different social locations. This is to monitor progress and effectiveness, or otherwise, of policies. Increasingly, policy bodies seeking to end violence have become more explicit in their calls for relevant data, statistics and indicators. These bodies include the UN and its agencies, regional governance entities and states. Drawing on their legally defined mandates, they have been articulating their principles within policies designed to end violence, or at least specific forms of violence.

There are a series of international legal instruments that have called for the ending of violence, in particular gender-based violence against women, at UN and regional levels. These legal instruments are binding on states that sign them; a process shaped by international courts.

The goal of ending violence is not new. After Fascism, the Holocaust and the Second World War (1939–45), several international and transnational entities were established as part of a wideranging peace project, including the UN, the Council of Europe and the EU.

However, the goal of measuring violence in a way that distinguishes between women and men *is* new.

International legal instruments

The relevant international legal instruments include: the 1948 *Universal Declaration of Human Rights*[27]; the 1979 *Convention on the Elimination of Discrimination against Women* (CEDAW)[28] and General Recommendation 19 on violence[29]; the 1993 UN *Declaration on the Elimination of Violence against Women* (DEVAW)[30], the 1995 *Beijing Platform for Action*[31] and the *Palermo Convention on Trafficking in Persons*[32]. The work of UN agencies is also significant, especially the UN Office for Drugs and Crime (UNODC)[33], UN Women[34] and the World Health Organization (WHO)[35], which are mandated to implement such legal instruments.

While there are further international legal instruments and tribunals that specifically address crimes of violence in war and conflict zones, this book is focused on non–conflict zones; where there is a significant

---

[27] UN (1948) *Universal Declaration of Human Rights.* www.un.org/en/universal-declaration-human-rights/ [November 2016].

[28] UN (1979) *Convention on the Elimination of Discrimination Against Women.* www.un.org/womenwatch/daw/cedaw/text/econvention.htm [November 2016].

[29] UN (1992) *Convention on the Elimination of Discrimination against Women, General Recommendation 19.* www.un.org/womenwatch/daw/cedaw/recommendations/recomm.htm#top [November 2016].

[30] UN General Assembly (1993) *Declaration on the Elimination of Violence against Women, UN General Assembly 1993 Resolution A/RES, 48/104.* www.un.org/documents/ga/res/48/a48r104.htm [November 2016].

[31] UN (1995) *Beijing Platform for Action.* www.un.org/womenwatch/daw/beijing/platform/ [November 2016].

[32] UN (2000) Protocol to Prevent, Suppress and Punish Trafficking in Persons, Especially Women and Children, Supplementing the United Nations Convention against Transnational Organized Crime, 2237 UNTS 391, opened for signature 12 December 2000, entered into force 25 December 2003. https://treaties.un.org/doc/Publication/UNTS/Volume%202237/v2237.pdf [November 2016].

[33] UNODC (2015) *International Classification of Crimes for Statistical Purposes.* Version 1.0. Geneva, UNODC.

[34] UN Women. www.unwomen.org/en/about-us/about-un-women [November 2016].

[35] WHO (2016) *Violence* www.who.int/topics/violence/en/ [November 2016].

difference for the same form of violence in a conflict zone, this is addressed.

United Nations

The goal to end violence, including gender-based violence, is articulated in the UN Sustainable Development Goals (SDGs)[36]. The UN 2030 Agenda for Sustainable Development[37] established 17 SDGs and 169 Targets through agreement by UN Member States in September 2015. Violence and gender are threaded through the Agenda: 'We are determined to foster peaceful, just and inclusive societies which are free from fear and violence. There can be no sustainable development without peace and no peace without sustainable development' (Paragraph 5) and 'The systematic mainstreaming of a gender perspective in the implementation of the Agenda is crucial' (Paragraph 20).

The SDGs to end violence, including violence against women, draw on the UN's aforementioned legal and policy commitments. The 17 SDGs build on the progress made by the UN Millennium Development Goals[38]; they each have several specified targets, which are intended to have numerical indicators so progress against them can be measured[39]. At least two SDGs are relevant to violence. These are SDG 16: 'Promote peaceful and inclusive societies for sustainable development, provide access to justice for all and build effective, accountable and inclusive institutions at all levels' and SDG 5: 'Achieve gender equality and empower all women and girls'. Within SDG 16 are Target 16.1: 'Significantly reduce all forms of violence and

---

[36]   UN (2015) *Sustainable Development Goals*. https://sustainabledevelopment. un.org/?menu=1300 [November 2016].

[37]   UN (2015) *Transforming our World: the 2030 Agenda for Sustainable Development*. https://sustainabledevelopment.un.org/post2015/transformingourworld [November 2016].

[38]   UN (2015) *Millennium Development Goals*. www.un.org/millenniumgoals/ [November 2016].

[39]   UN (2015) *Sustainable Development Goals*. https://sustainabledevelopment. un.org/?menu=1300 [November 2016].

related death rates everywhere' and Target 16.3: 'Promote the rule of law at the national and international levels and ensure equal access to justice for all'. Within SDG 5 are Target 5.2: 'Eliminate all forms of violence against all women and girls in the public and private spheres, including trafficking and sexual and other types of exploitation' and Target 5.3: 'Eliminate all harmful practices, such as child, early and forced marriage and female genital mutilation'. SDG 5 includes a target to eliminate all forms of violence against women and girls by 2030, which requires the UN Statistical Commission to develop indicators to monitor progress during 2016.

There are several UN–related developments concerning indicators. The Friends of the Chair of the UN Statistical Commission recommended nine core indicators to measure the extent of violence against women[40]. The UN Division for the Advancement of Women published a model framework for legislation and associated policies

[40] UN Statistical Commission (2010) *Report on the Meeting of the Friends of the Chair of the United Nations Statistical Commission on Statistical Indicators on Violence against Women*, Aguascalientes, Mexico, 9–11 December 2009. www.un.org/womenwatch/daw/vaw/IssuesFocus/Report-of-the-Meeting-of-the-Friends-of-the-Chair-February-2010.pdf [November 2016]. The nine core indicators are:

1. Total and age specific rate of women subjected to physical violence in the last 12 months by severity of violence, relationship to the perpetrator and frequency.
2. Total and age specific rate of women subjected to physical violence during lifetime by severity of violence, relationship to the perpetrator and frequency.
3. Total and age specific rate of women subjected to sexual violence in the last 12 months by severity of violence, relationship to the perpetrator and frequency.
4. Total and age specific rate of women subjected to sexual violence during lifetime by severity of violence, relationship to the perpetrator and frequency.
5. Total and age specific rate of ever-partnered women subjected to sexual and/or physical violence by current or former intimate partner in the last 12 months by frequency.
6. Total and age specific rate of ever-partnered women subjected to sexual and/or physical violence by current or former intimate partner during lifetime by frequency.
7. Total and age specific rate of women subjected to psychological violence in the past 12 months by the intimate partner.
8. Total and age specific rate of women subjected to economic violence in the past 12 months by the intimate partner.
9. Total and age specific rate of women subjected to female genital mutilation.

on violence against women[41]. This offers a list of desirable legislation and associated policies (including implementation and protection of victims) that can be used to identify legal and related policy progress, though it is not a list of indicators.

UN Women has suggested a number of indicators, including several pertaining to violence against women and girls[42]. These include the proportion of women (and girls) who have been subject to: specific forms of violence (distinguishing between violence from current/former intimate partners and from others) (Target 5.2), harmful practices, including child marriage and Female Genital Mutilation (FGM) (Target 5.3) and physical and sexual harassment (Target 11.7). UN Women simultaneously supports the mainstreaming approach – 'a systematic disaggregation by sex of all relevant indicators across all goals and targets is needed' – and seeks, in association with the UNODC, gender disaggregated indicators on trafficking in human beings (Target 5.2) and homicide (Target 16.1).

Three differently gendered approaches to measuring violence, including violence against women, can be found among the UN agencies: gender-invisible universalism, a focus on women and gender mainstreaming. The UNODC, in cooperation with Eurostat, led the creation of a new International Classification of Crime for Statistical Purposes (ICCS)[43], which includes violent crime. Gender is invisible in the main four tiers of the coding scheme, completion of which is compulsory; it is present only in optional secondary tags about context. UN Women and the UN Statistics Commission have focused on violence against women, exploring ways of measuring the extent

---

[41]   UN Division for the Advancement of Women (2010) *Handbook for Legislation on Violence against Women.* www.un.org/womenwatch/daw/vaw/handbook/Handbook%20for%20legislation%20on%20violence%20against%20women.pdf [November 2016].

[42]   UN Women (2015) *Monitoring Gender Equality and the Empowerment of Women and Girls in the 2030 Agenda for Sustainable Development: Opportunities and Challenges.* http://www2.unwomen.org/~/media/headquarters/attachments/sections/library/publications/2015/indicatorpaper-en-final.pdf?v=1&d=20150921T140212 [November 2016].

[43]   UNODC (2015) *Op cit.* Footnote 33.

of this violence in surveys asked of women only[44], such as those of the WHO[45]. Yet, gender mainstreaming is UN policy, importantly developed in the Beijing Platform for Action[46], found in many parts of the UN system – including, as mentioned, UN Women.

Regional legal instruments

The UN legal instruments have been developed in global regions in the Council of Europe, for example the Council of Europe *Convention on Preventing and Combating Violence against Women and Domestic Violence*, known as the *Istanbul Convention*[47], the *Inter-American Convention on the Prevention, Punishment and Eradication of Violence against Women 'Convention of Belem do Para'*[48] and the *Protocol to the African Charter on Human and Peoples' Rights on the Rights of Women in Africa*[49]. There are further relevant Conventions, including those concerning trafficking in human beings, such as the Council of Europe *Convention on Action against Trafficking in Human Beings*[50].

[44] UN Women (2015) *Op cit.* Footnote 42; UN Department for Economic and Social Affairs (2014) Guidelines for Producing Statistics on Violence Against Women: Statistical Surveys.

[45] WHO (2005) *WHO Multi-Country Study on Women's Health and Domestic Violence against Women*. Geneva, WHO.

[46] UN (1995) *Beijing Platform for Action*. www.un.org/womenwatch/daw/beijing/platform/ [November 2016].

[47] Council of Europe (2011) *Convention on Preventing and Combating Violence against Women and Domestic Violence (Istanbul Convention)*. https://rm.coe.int/CoERMPublicCommonSearchServices/DisplayDCTMContent?documentId=090000168046031c [November 2016].

[48] Organisation of American States (1994) *Inter-American Convention on the Prevention, Punishment and Eradication of Violence against Women* 'Convention of Belem do Para'. www.oas.org/juridico/english/treaties/a-61.html [November 2016].

[49] African Commission on Human and Peoples' Rights (1995) *Protocol to the African Charter on Human and Peoples' Rights on the Rights of Women in Africa*. www.achpr.org/files/instruments/women-protocol/achpr_instr_proto_women_eng.pdf [November 2016].

[50] Council of Europe (2005) *Convention on Action against Trafficking in Human Beings*. http://www.coe.int/en/web/anti-human-trafficking [November 2016].

Council of Europe

The Council of Europe *Istanbul Convention on Preventing and Combating Violence Against Women and Domestic Violence* names many forms of gender-based violence and places obligations on those states that have ratified it[51].

Article 11 of the *Istanbul Convention* requires such states to collect administrative and survey data and conduct research on violence against women[52]. This includes the production of 'conviction rates' (Article 11.1.b). In addition, Article 10 states that data collection is to be coordinated by a national body. To comply with the Convention, Member States that have ratified it will need to collect data on violence against women as follows (Article 11):

1. For the purposes of the implementation of this Convention, Parties shall undertake to:
   (a) collect disaggregated relevant statistical data at regular intervals on cases of all forms of violence covered by the scope of this Convention;
   (b) support research in the field of all forms of violence covered by the scope of this Convention in order to study its root causes and effects, incidences and conviction rates, as well as the efficacy of measures taken to implement this Convention.
2. Parties shall endeavour to conduct population-based surveys at regular intervals to assess the prevalence of and trends in all forms of violence covered by the scope of this Convention.
3. Parties shall provide the group of experts, as referred to in Article 66 of this Convention, with the information collected pursuant to this article in order to stimulate international co-operation and enable international benchmarking.

---

[51] Council of Europe (2011) *Op cit.* Footnote 47.
[52] Council of Europe (2016) *Ensuring Data Collection and Research on Violence against Women and Domestic Violence: Article 11 of the Istanbul Convention.* Prepared by S. Walby.

4. Parties shall ensure that the information collected pursuant to this article is available to the public.

The *Istanbul Convention* was developed by the Council of Europe under the auspices of the *European Convention on Human Rights*. The Council of Europe, of which 47 states are members, is the guardian of the *European Convention of Human Rights* (ECHR)[53]. This is the European interpretation of the UN *Universal Declaration of Human Rights*, which is implemented through the jurisprudence of the European Court of Human Rights (ECtHR)[54] in Strasbourg. While the ECHR was originally understood as a universalistic approach to human rights in which gender was invisible, the development of the jurisprudence of the ECtHR has in recent years explicitly named gender-based violence as within its remit[55]. The *Istanbul Convention* foregrounds the gender dimension using a dual focus on women and on domestic violence.

It provides an important listing of forms of violence and coercion underpinned by international law. Additional forms of violence noted in the other regional conventions are 'trafficking in persons'[56], 'forced prostitution' and 'kidnapping'. The forms of violence named in the *Istanbul Convention* are:

- *Physical violence*: 'committing acts of physical violence against another person' (Article 35). The category 'physical violence' includes both lethal and non-lethal physical violence.
- *Sexual violence, including rape:* '*a* engaging in non-consensual vaginal, anal or oral penetration of a sexual nature of the body of another

[53] European Court of Human Rights (ECtHR) (1953) *European Convention on Human Rights*. Strasburg, ECtHR. www.echr.coe.int/Documents/Convention_ENG.pdf [November 2016].

[54] ECtHR (1953) *Op cit*. Footnote 53.

[55] Council of Europe (2016) *Ensuring Data Collection and Research on Violence against Women and Domestic Violence – Article 11 of the Istanbul Convention*. Prepared by Sylvia Walby. https://rm.coe.int/CoERMPublicCommonSearchServices/DisplayDCTMContent?documentId=0900001680640efc [November 2016].

[56] While trafficking in human beings is not specifically covered in the *Istanbul Convention*, it is the subject of the separate treaty of the Council of Europe: the 2005 Convention on Action against Trafficking in Human Beings.

person with any bodily part or object; *b* engaging in other non-consensual acts of a sexual nature with a person; *c* causing another person to engage in non-consensual acts of a sexual nature with a third person. Consent must be given voluntarily as the result of the person's free will assessed in the context of the surrounding circumstances' (Article 36).

- *Forced marriage:* 'forcing an adult or a child to enter into a marriage' (Article 37).
- *FGM:* '*a* excising, infibulating or performing any other mutilation to the whole or any part of a woman's labia majora, labia minora or clitoris; *b* coercing or procuring a woman to undergo any of the acts listed in point *a*; *c* inciting, coercing or procuring a girl to undergo any of the acts listed in point *a*' (Article 38).
- *Forced abortion and forced sterilisation:* '*a* performing an abortion on a woman without her prior and informed consent; *b* performing surgery which has the purpose or effect of terminating a woman's capacity to naturally reproduce without her prior and informed consent or understanding of the procedure' (Article 39).
- *Psychological violence:* 'seriously impairing a person's psychological integrity through coercion or threats' (Article 33).
- *Stalking:* 'repeatedly engaging in threatening conduct directed at another person, causing her or him to fear for her or his safety' (Article 34).
- *Sexual harassment:* 'any form of unwanted verbal, non-verbal or physical conduct of a sexual nature with the purpose or effect of violating the dignity of a person, in particular when creating an intimidating hostile, degrading, humiliating or offensive environment' (Article 40).

European Union

In the EU, interest in developing better data on violent crime including gender-based violence is found in the European Commission[57]; the European Parliament[58]; the European Council of Ministers[59]; the Equal Opportunities Committee[60], the European Institute for Gender Equality (EIGE)[61] and the Fundamental Rights Agency (FRA). This development has been enabled by the extension in powers at the EU level in the area of security, justice and freedom in the Treaty of

[57] European Commission (EC) (2010) *Strategy for Equality between Women and Men 2010–2015.* Brussels, EC; European Commission (EC) (2016) *Strategic Engagement on Gender Equality 2016-2019.* Brussels, EC.

[58] European Parliament (2009) *Elimination of Violence against Women.* P7_TA (2009) 0098 European Parliament Resolution. http://www.europarl.europa.eu/sides/getDoc.do?pubRef=-//EP//TEXT+TA+P7-TA-2009-0098+0+DOC+XML+V0//EN [November 2016]; European Parliament (2014) *Motion for a European Parliament Resolution on the EU Strategy for Equality between Women and Men Post 2015* (2014/2152(INI)).

[59] European Union (EU) (2010) *Council Conclusions on the Eradication of Violence against Women in the European Union.* 3000th Employment and Social Policy Council meeting, Brussels, 8 March 2010. www.consilium.europa.eu/uedocs/cms_data/docs/pressdata/en/lsa/113226.pdf [November 2016]; EU (2011) *Council Conclusions on European Pact for Gender Equality* (2011–2020). 2011/C 115/02. http://eur-lex.europa.eu/LexUriServ/LexUriServ.do?uri=OJ:C:2011:15 5:0010:0013:EN:PDF [November 2016]; EU (2012) *Council Conclusions on Combatting Violence against Women and the Provision of Support Services for Victims of Domestic Violence.* 3206th Employment, Social Policy, Health and Consumer Affairs Council meeting, Brussels, 6 December 2012; EU (2014) Council Conclusions 'Preventing and Combatting all Forms of Violence against Women and Girls, including Female Genital Mutilation' Justice and Home Affairs Council meeting, Luxembourg. http://ec.europa.eu/justice/gender-equality/files/jha_violence_girls_council_conclusions_2014_en.pdf [November 2016].

[60] Advisory Committee on Equal Opportunities for Women and Men (2014) *Opinion on Data Collection on Violence against Women.* http://ec.europa.eu/justice/gender-equality/files/opinions_advisory_committee/141126_opinion_data_vaw_en.pdf [November 2016].

[61] European Institute for Gender Equality (EIGE) (2015) *Strategic Framework on Violence Against Women, 2015–2018.* http://eige.europa.eu/sites/default/files/documents/amended_vaw_strategic_framework_2015-2018_approved_20160610.pdf [November 2016].

Lisbon[62] – now articulated through Directives and Resolutions[63] – and the Stockholm programme[64]. These include a range of requirements concerning data. For example, the 2012 Victims Directive Article 28 places an obligation on Member States to provide data to the European Commission on how victims have accessed their rights[65].

There have been repeated calls in the EU for indicators. The EU Presidencies have suggested indicators for violence against women in the context of the EU's commitment to the Beijing Platform for Action, addressing the provision of support services for victims of domestic violence, sexual harassment in the workplace and violence against women[66]. The EIGE includes violence against women in its Gender Equality Index published in 2015[67], but the poor quality of the measurement framework and data used ensures that, as a comparison between countries, it is – at best – meaningless. There are currently no reliable indicators of differences in the rate of violence or gender-based violence between Member States of the EU.

---

[62] Walby, S. (2014) *European Added Value of a Directive on Combating Violence Against Women.* Annex 2, Part 2: Legal Perspectives. Brussels, European Parliament Value Added Unit. www.europarl.europa.eu/RegData/etudes/etudes/join/2013/504467/IPOL-JOIN_ET(2013)504467(ANN02)_EN.pdf [November 2016].

[63] European Parliament (2011) *Resolution on Priorities and Outline of a New EU Policy Framework to Fight Violence against Women.* http://publications.europa.eu/en/publication-detail/-/publication/9debe9f2-0c8a-11e2-8e28-01aa75ed71a1/language-en [November 2016]; European Parliament (2014) *Resolution of 25 February 2014 with Recommendations to the Commission on Combating Violence Against Women* (2013/2004(INL)). www.europarl.europa.eu/sides/getDoc.do?pubRef=-//EP//NONSGML+TA+P7-TA-2014-0126+0+DOC+PDF+V0//EN [November 2016].

[64] EU (2010) The Stockholm Programme: An Open and Secure Europe Serving and Protecting Citizens. 2010/C 115/01. http://eur-lex.europa.eu/LexUriServ/LexUriServ.do?uri=OJ:C:2010:115:0001:0038:EN:PDF [November 2016].

[65] For example, EU Directive 2012/29 *Establishing minimum standards on the rights, support and protection of victims of crime.* http://eur-lex.europa.eu/LexUriServ/LexUriServ.do?uri=OJ:L:2012:315:0057:0073:EN:PDF [November 2016].

[66] European Commission (2015) *Beijing Platform for Action.* http://ec.europa.eu/justice/gender-equality/tools/statistics-indicators/platform-action/index_en.htm [November 2016].

[67] EIGE (2015) *Gender Equality Index.* http://eige.europa.eu/sites/default/files/documents/mh0415169enn.pdf [November 2016].

The EU practices three differently gendered approaches to measuring violence: gender-invisible, women-only and gender mainstreaming. Gender invisibility is the consequence of Eurostat adopting the UNODC ICCS to organise its collection of administrative data on crime, including violent crime, since this does not include gender in its mandatory data collection. Women-only is the approach of the FRA in its survey on violence against women only[68] and the EIGE, which names its strategy in this field as concerning violence against women[69]. Gender mainstreaming is the official European Commission approach to policy on gender issues[70], which draws its authority from EU Treaties; most recently the Treaty of Lisbon[71], which has been implemented in a series of EU Strategies on equality between women and men[72].

UK

In 2016, the UK Statistics Authority is reviewing the national framework for statistics on crime and justice[73] while the Office for National Statistics is reviewing its measurement of domestic abuse. In

[68] Fundamental Rights Agency (FRA) (2014) *Violence against Women: An EU-Wide Survey*. http://fra.europa.eu/en/publication/2014/violence-against-women-eu-wide-survey-main-results-report [November 2016].

[69] *EIGE (2015) Strategic Framework on Violence against Women 2015-2018*. Vilnius, European Institute for Gender Equality. http://eige.europa.eu/rdc/eige-publications/strategic-framework-violence-against-women-2015-2018 [November 2016].

[70] European Commission (2016) *Strategic Engagement for Gender Equality, 2016–2019*. http://ec.europa.eu/justice/gender-equality/document/files/strategic_engagement_en.pdf [November 2016].

[71] EU (2006) *Treaty on the Functioning of the European Union* http://eur-lex.europa.eu/legal-content/EN/TXT/PDF/?uri=CELEX:12012E/TXT&from=EN [November 2016].

[72] European Commission (2010) *Op cit*. Footnote 57; European Commission (2016) *Op cit*. Footnote 70.

[73] UK Statistics Authority (2016) *UK Statistics Authority Business Plan: 2016–2020*. www.statisticsauthority.gov.uk/wp-content/uploads/2016/04/UKSA-Business-Plan-0416-0320.pdf [November 2016]. 'We will carry out strategic reviews of cross-cutting issues or thematic groups of statistics which aim to maximise the value of official statistics to the UK public. During 2016 ... [C] ontinued drive to improve Crime and justice statistics and health statistics' (p.28).

mainstream police-recorded crime statistics, gender is almost invisible, while moves towards the 'flagging' of domestic abuse vary across the 43 police force areas, thereby precluding the possibility of a national picture[74]. Despite its collection of gender-disaggregated data from respondents, the headline statistics of the Crime Survey for England and Wales (CSEW) make gender almost invisible, while domestic abuse is treated as a separate field with a different methodology that renders it incomparable to the main statistical series on violent crime.

Conclusions

Most states, as well as the UN, Council of Europe and European Union, now have law and policy to reduce – if not to end – violence, especially gender-based violence against women. The measurement of violence and its gender dimensions are increasingly important aspects of the developments needed to achieve this goal.

[74] Her Majesty's Inspectorate of Constabulary (HMIC) (2014) *Everyone's Business: Improving the Police Response to Domestic Abuse*. Review of Domestic Violence Statistics. www.justiceinspectorates.gov.uk/hmic/wp-content/uploads/2014/04/improving-the-police-response-to-domestic-abuse.pdf [November 2016].

CONCEPTUALISING VIOLENCE AND GENDER

Introduction

Producing a coherent and consistent measurement framework requires a coherent and consistent conceptualisation of violence and gender. This conceptual framework is anchored in the principles embedded in international legal instruments and developed through reviews of research.

Because international legal instruments mobilise general concepts and principles, this approach is not the same as identifying violence with specific national criminal codes. The definition of violence depends on the location of the boundary between violence and not-violence. This depends on the understanding of the nature of the act (and intention) and the harm (and non-consent), although not all approaches have considered all these elements to be essential. In addition, it is necessary to address variations in repetition, duration and seriousness. Consistent units of measurement (event, victim and perpetrator) and technical counting rules are also essential for the measurement framework.

Competing approaches to conceptualising gender relations determine whether the measurement framework for violence makes gender invisible, focuses on women or mainstreams gender. Gender relations saturate, shape or inflect many aspects of violence; they are not only its context. Taking gender into account is not only an issue of whether victims and perpetrators are individual men or women. Five different dimensions of gender relations relevant to violence are identified here. These include the gender-saturated relationship between perpetrator and victim, any sexual aspect to the violence and any gender motivation of the perpetrator.

What is violence?

The location of the boundary between violence and not-violence is here ontologically anchored in international law and deepened with research findings. The focus of the measurement framework is illegal violence. Violence that is legal (because it is sanctioned by states and international law) is not the focus of this measurement framework, since it requires different methods; it is addressed only briefly. Locating the boundary between violence and not-violence includes considerations of actions (including intention) and harms (including non-consent), physicality and repetition, duration and seriousness. There are technical issues concerning the unit of measurement and recording and counting rules. Variations by form of violence and policy field are considered in subsequent chapters.

Actions (and intentions) and harms (and non-consent)

Violence is a kind of social relationship between perpetrator and victim in the sense that both perpetrator and victim are necessary to the event. Actions (and intentions) and harms (and non-consent) are all necessary to define violence. The concept of crime also requires all these components.

The perpetrator performs the action. The perpetrator is usually an individual person, but may be a group of people or other collective. The action may be intended to harm or not, or may be intended to cause a different degree of harm from that achieved. The intention to perform an action that will cause harm is part of the action. This means that even when the action is not completed or does not cause the harm intended, it still counts.

There are five categories of non-completion of an intended violent action that are treated within criminal justice systems as crimes: threats to commit violence; aiding/abetting/accessory; accomplice; conspiracy/planning; and incitement. We recommend following the UNODC[75], American Academy of Sciences[76], United Nations Surveys on Crime Trends and the Operations of Criminal Justice Systems (UN–CTS) and European Sourcebook[77] in including these as violent crimes while labelling them clearly as not completed. This is consistent with research findings that the characteristics of attempted and completed homicides are very similar[78]. It would be appropriate if statistics produced by Eurostat and the World Health Organization (WHO) were brought into alignment with this.

The harm is that done to the victim. Harm is a detriment to wellbeing. It is most likely to be a physical injury, but may be mental or psychological. Harm is usually understood to have occurred if the victim did not consent. The interpretation of 'consent' in law is discussed further in relation to rape in Chapter Four.

Actions alone are not sufficient to define either violence or crime. Distinctions between forms of violence and between crimes are defined through specific combinations of actions (and intentions) and harms (and non-consent). The action and the harm are often in alignment, when a proportionately harsher action causes a proportionately more devastating harm – but on occasions they are not. When there is alignment between actions, harms and intentions, measurement and analysis is much simpler than when there is divergence between them. If they are in alignment, then one of the three can act as a proxy for

[75] UNODC (2015) *Op cit.* Footnote 33.
[76] Reiss, A. and Roth, J. (eds) (1994) *Understanding and Preventing Violence.* Washington, National Academy Press.
[77] Smit, P., de Jong, R. and Bijleveld, C. (2012) 'Homicide data in Europe: definitions, sources and statistics', in Liem, M. and Pridemore, W. (eds) *Handbook of European Homicide Research*: 5.
[78] Bikleveld, C. and Smit, P. (2006) 'Homicide in the Netherlands: on the structuring of homicide typologies', *Homicide Studies*, 10: 195–219.

the other two; if not, then they cannot. While there is often a popular assumption of alignment between actions (and intentions) and harms (and non-consent), criminal law often allows for nuance where this alignment is absent. For example, in relation to the action of killing (generally termed 'homicide'), the law in most countries makes distinctions according to the degree of intention to kill: whether it was deliberately planned; intended, but on the spur of the moment; or not intended to have such serious consequences. In relation to the action of assault, there are degrees of severity of the crime that focus on the level of harm caused: whether there is a physical injury or not and whether this is serious/grievous or minor/actual. The consent or lack of consent of the victim matters; the capacity to consent is affected by age (adult/minor), intoxication through use of alcohol or drugs and the abuse of authority, as well as physical force, threat or coercion.

Forms of measurement that focus on only one aspect of action, intention, harm or non-consent are partial and should be rejected. Examples include the measurement of domestic violence through actions alone and the measurement of violence focused on harms without agents.

The Conflict Tactics Scale (CTS) developed by Gelles and Straus[79] focuses on actions only, excluding harms and intentions. The instrument asks about a series of actions; it does not include the intention of the perpetrator or the harms caused to the victim in the same scale. Hence, some actions are included that are not crimes because there was no intention to harm[80]. Data collected using the CTS is not compatible with data collected using crime codes. Further, the gender asymmetric harm of a given action (the same action from a man to a woman typically causes more injuries than the same action from a woman to a man)[81] is not included in the scale. In

[79]   Straus, M. and Gelles, R. (eds) (1999) *Physical Violence in American Families.* 2nd ed. New Brunswick, Transaction Publishers.

[80]   Ackerman, J. (2016) 'Over-reporting Intimate Partner Violence in Australian survey research', *British Journal of Criminology*, 56: 646–67.

[81]   Walby, S. and Allen, J. (2004) *Domestic Violence, Sexual Assault and Stalking: Findings from the British Crime Survey.* Home Office Research Study 276. London, Home Office: 37–8.

modified form, the scale has been used in many specialised violence against women surveys, including those of the Fundamental Rights Agency (FRA) EU-wide survey[82]. We conclude that the CTS is not an appropriate instrument to measure violence, since it does not take harms and intentions into account. Other surveys share the exclusive focus on actions rather than harms, although they differ from the CTS in other respects; for example, the WHO multi-country surveys on violence against women[83].

Galtung's[84] concept of structural violence includes harms but not intentions and no exclusions to the possible range of actions. He focuses on social structures rather than individual actions that lead to unnecessary death. These unnecessary deaths may be a result of a variety of causes, from famine to poverty. Unwanted physical contact violence is not a significant part of his account. The level of analysis does not include individuals with their actions and intentions. He is interested in the wider, deeper, more abstract level of the societal production of harms. Galtung's analysis underpins the definitions of indirect and direct violence proposed by the European Institute for Gender Equality (EIGE)[85] in their Gender Equality Index. Consequently, the EIGE includes an extremely wide range of phenomena as 'indirect violence', extending as far as gender stereotypes in culture. It is hard to find anything that the EIGE considers to *not* be indirect violence; that is, there is no effective distinction between violence and not-violence. For practical purposes, this is not useful, since by blocking the separate identification of violence from other aspects of gender inequality it prevents any effective analysis of the relationship between violence and gender inequality. Investigating the relationship between social systems and violence is an important part of a research programme, but is not definitional. While variations in social structure are relevant

[82]   FRA (2014) *Op cit.* Footnote 68.
[83]   WHO (2005) *Op cit.* Footnote 45.
[84]   Galtung, J. (1969) 'Violence, peace and peace research', *Journal of Peace Research*, 16: 167–91.
[85]   EIGE (2015) *Op cit.* Footnote 61.

to explaining patterns of violence, they should not be treated as part of the definition of violence.

We conclude that actions (and intentions) and harm (and non-consent) are together necessary for the definition of violence for use in the measurement framework.

Physicality and the threshold of violence

Is physicality – involving the body, the corporeal, contact and touch – an essential component of violence? Or is it sufficient for the action to be abusive, coercive or controlling and/or the harm to be an injury or detriment to mental wellbeing or health? These borderlands especially include non-physical coercion, threats, attempts and other non-completed or indirect actions.

The social science literature is divided into support for a narrow or a wide definition. Among those that use a wide definition, Bourdieu[86] introduces the concept of 'symbolic violence', thereby extending the use of the term 'violence' to include cultural power. This would mean that it is not possible to distinguish the distinctiveness of violence as a form of power. Indeed, it can even lead to the aforementioned inclusion of gender stereotypes as a form of violence[87], thereby preventing an analysis of the relationship between culture and violence. The alternative approach is to identify violence as a specific practice with its own modalities and rhythms, which is not reducible to anything else. This approach, adopted for example by Collins[88], enables a clear separation between violence and its causes and thus the investigation of the relations between them. Non-violent forms of coercion are not reducible to violent forms of coercion, but they may be connected.

Non-physical coercion may or may not result in injury to mental health; it includes repeated intrusive communications, stalking, sexual

---

[86]   Bourdieu, P. (1991) *Language and Symbolic Power*. Cambridge, Polity Press.
[87]   EIGE (2015) *Op cit*. Footnote 61.
[88]   Randall, C. (2008) *Violence*. Princeton, Princeton University Press.

and gender harassment and trafficking in human beings. 'Violence' is here restricted to those events that involve physical contact (including non-consented sexual contact and contact via a weapon) from the perpetrator or physical harm to the wellbeing of the victim. Other forms of criminal coercion also require measurement in a framework, which should be comparable with a measurement framework for violence, but violence and not-violence are not the same and should not be conflated in the same definition. Coercion may be subject to criminal sanction even when there is not a physical component; as such, the boundary between crime/not-crime is not the same as physical/not-physical. Several gendered forms of coercion straddle the physical/non-physical boundary; in particular, stalking, sexual and gender harassment, a course of coercive conduct by an intimate partner or family member and trafficking in human beings. Domestic abuse includes physical and non-physical acts, while domestic violence may be defined more narrowly. These boundary cases are discussed in more detail in Chapter Four.

Non-completed and indirect includes threats to commit violence, attempts at violence that are not completed and aiding, abetting, inciting or conspiring with others to commit violence. Criminal justice systems have developed practices to address the various degrees of completion and indirectness of criminal violence. There are forms of technical guidance and rules that specify these in detail in many countries. The harmonisation of these practices between countries remains an issue to be resolved. This is most advanced, but not finished, in the case of homicide.

Seriousness, repetition and duration

Variations in violence can be found in relation to its seriousness, repetition and duration. These apply separately to the actions of the perpetrator and the harms experienced by the victim. They may or may not be in alignment or proportionate.

The *seriousness* of the action is aligned with, or proportionate to, the harm to the victim. In particular, this is gendered, in that the same action tends to generate more severe harms when performed by a man rather than a woman[89]. Lethal violence is more reliably measured than non-lethal violence and physical injury is more reliably measured than non-physical forms of harm. The intention of the perpetrator affects the seriousness of the event, whether premeditated; with an aggravating motivation (for example, a hate crime or gendered motivation); in the heat of the moment, reckless or accidental.

The action may be *repeated*. This challenges the assumption of alignment between one perpetrator, one victim and one event. Repetition is particularly a feature of domestic violence (and therefore of violence perpetrated against women) and forms of threat and coercion that accumulate to constitute violence; it is less common for violence committed by strangers to be repeated and hence is a more important feature of violent crime against women[90]. Repetition means an accumulation of harm in high-frequency victims, who are disproportionately women. Yet, the default assumption in measuring violence is still one victim, one perpetrator, one event. Repeated acts should be counted to ensure that this distinctive gendered feature of some forms of violence is captured rather than disregarded. The repetition of acts that might not individually count as violence, but which in their repetition constitute an ever-increasing threat of harm, means that they should be included in the concept of violence. This is the defining feature of stalking and harassment.

The *duration* of the action may take the form of repeated discrete incidents of violence; the harm may be experienced as a continuous state of fear. Such lack of alignment of the temporality for perpetrator and victim poses challenges for a measurement framework. This is mitigated if the unit of measurement explicitly takes this into account; for example, by not conflating the perpetrator, victim and event into one unit, but rather separately accounting for them (discussed shortly). Issues of repetition and duration are further addressed in the discussion

---

[89]   Walby, S. and Allen, J. (2004) *Op cit*. Footnote 81.

[90]   Walby, S., Towers, J. and Francis, B. (2014) 'Mainstreaming domestic and gender-based violence in sociology and the criminology of violence', *Sociological Review*, 62: 187–214.

of domestic violence in the next chapter in relation to the concepts of a 'continuum'[91] and of 'coercive control'[92]. We conclude that the measurement framework needs to include a count of repetitions, notwithstanding the different temporalities of actions and harms.

Variations in the type of violence emerge from these variations in the nature, severity, duration and repetition of the actions of the perpetrator and the harms experienced by the victim. These tend to cluster into forms of violence recognised in law as different crimes; new types may emerge and old types be rejected through public debate. Variation in forms of violence include homicide/femicide, rape, domestic violence and Female Genital Mutilation (FGM), as well as (but not fully developed here) stalking/harassment, war and violence against civilians in conflict zones, including war crimes (such as genocide) and rape as a weapon of war.

Units of measurement

Measurement requires the identification of the relevant unit. These are events, victims and perpetrators. While conventionally there is an assumption of one perpetrator and one victim for each event, in practice these are not so simply aligned, as in the case of domestic violence where there are multiple events from one perpetrator to one victim. It is important to ensure that measurement uses all three units of events, victims and perpetrators.

Measuring the treatment of violence in the work of public services requires both the number of events (how many crimes, or perhaps how many visits to a particular service) in a fixed period of time (such as a year) and the number of victims. Violence can have a complex temporality. The physical act may take place over a short space of time and it may be repeated; but the impact can last a much longer time, including the injury and harm to physical and/or mental health,

---

[91] Kelly, L. (1988) *Surviving Sexual Violence*. Cambridge, Polity Press.
[92] Schechter, S. (1982) *Women and Male Violence*. New York, Harper Collins; Stark, E. (2009) *Coercive Control: How Men Entrap Women in Personal Life*. Oxford, Oxford University Press.

fear and consequent coercion and control. Most services and most data collection mechanisms use one of these three units. Addressing gender-based violence requires using all three: events, victims and perpetrators. Measuring one is not a substitute for the others; all three are needed because they capture distinctly different aspects of the process of violence.

If there is to be successful mobilisation of all relevant public services, there will need to be greater compatibility in units of measurement. For example, if there are to be routinely available conviction rates (discussed shortly), this requires the same unit of measurement throughout the criminal justice system. There are two approaches to this. One is to assert the dominance of one of the three categories. The other is to collect information in all three of the measurement units. The first would be difficult to achieve in a consensual approach. The second would require cooperation around the shared goal of ending violence. It is interesting to note that, in practice, many agencies often have the information using the other units of measurement in narrative form in 'files', even if they do not abstract this information into their statistical systems. This would mean that the challenge is not the major one of organising new data collection, but rather the more modest one of mining the already collected data for the relevant information to upload into statistical systems. Likewise, surveys should collect information about events, victims and perpetrators and not be restricted to only one or two of these units of measurement.

Counting rules

Ensuring comparability and reliability of data recorded by administrative organisations (such as the police) requires the systematic application of technical 'counting rules' to determine what is counted, what is excluded and how many events (such as crimes) make up an incident.

Variations in counting practices between countries and agencies have regularly been found to reduce comparability[93]. Consistency is needed.

There are several issues over which counting rules are needed: the date attributed to the crime; the measurement (or counting) unit; whether an event is classified by its principal offence or all offences are counted; how offences by multiple perpetrators are counted; how offences by the same perpetrator against multiple victims are counted; and how multiple offences against the same victim continuing in time are counted. The UNODC[94] notes the first five of these six issues but declines to offer a solution, suggesting that 'the harmonisation of counting rules is best treated ... separately from the structure and application of the ICCS'. We offer solutions here, since the issues are too important to defer.

First, the date of the violent crime should be recorded as the date it took place, even if this needs to be estimated. The alternative of using the date when the crime was discovered risks distortion (as occurs, for example, when a serial offender is ultimately apprehended[95]).

Second, the simultaneous use of three measurement units (events, victims and perpetrators) at each data collection point prevents the potential complexities around multiple offenders, multiple crimes or multiple victims from arising. Third, each event should be classified by a principal offence. This requires a hierarchy of offences[96]. Stability

[93]   UNODC (2015) *Op cit.* Footnote 33; Aebi, M. (2008) 'Measuring the influence of statistical counting rules on cross-national differences in recorded crime', in Aromaa, K. and Heiskanen, M. (eds) *Crime and Criminal Justice Systems in Europe and North America 1995–2004*. Heldsinki, HEIUNI: 200–18; van Hoer, H. (2000) 'Crime statistics as constructs: the case of Swedish rape statistics', *European Journal on Criminal Policy and Research*, 8: 77–89.

[94]   UNODC (2015) *Op cit*: 106. Footnote 33.

[95]   Smith, J. (2002) *Death Disguised*. London, The Shipman Inquiry. www.gov.uk/government/uploads/system/uploads/attachment_data/file/273227/5854.pdf [November 2016].

[96]   Mosher, C., Miethe, T. and Philips, D. (2002) *The Miss-Measure of Crime*. Thousand Oaks, Sage.

in this hierarchy is desirable[97], lest it changes the number of certain types of offence[98].

Conclusions on the concept of violence

The drawing of the boundary between violence and not-violence in this proposed measurement framework is anchored in international law. Yet, the boundary between violence and not-violence can be hard to determine in practice. Violence involves the actions (and intentions) of the perpetrator and the harms to (and non-consent of) the victim. 'Violence' means events that involve the actual, intended or threatened, direct or indirect physical contact by the perpetrator or bodily harm to the victim. It depends on intentions as well as actions (especially in addressing incomplete actions), on the interpretation of the concept of harm (including non-consent) and on the significance of repetition. Incomplete actions are included within the concept of violence because of the significance of intention; hence, attempts and threatened actions are included. The concept of harm focuses on a reference to the body. Repetition is significant in increasing the threat and actuality of harm. There is a need for consistent technical and counting rules to implement these principles. The usefulness, coherence and consistency of the measurement framework and the use of three units of measurement by all data collectors – events, victims and perpetrators – should all be included.

Conceptualising gender

Gender is not external to violence but can structure the core characteristics of the event that is a kind of social relationship between perpetrator and victim. Gender relations may thus not only structure

[97]   Francis, B., Soothill, K. and Dittrich, R. (2001) 'A new approach for ranking "serious" offences: the use of paired-comparisons methodology', *British Journal of Criminology*, 41: 726–37.
[98]   Newburn, T. (2007) '"Tough on crime": penal policy in England and Wales', *Crime and Justice*, 36: 425–70.

the wider context and causation of violence, but also saturate or partially constitute its core aspects, including violent crime. Gender saturation may vary, requiring the identification of various relevant dimensions. Addressing the conceptualisation of gender relevant to violence requires first considering the extent and manner in which gender is made visible and second the identification of which dimensions of gender are to be made visible.

Gender visibility

There are three main approaches to gender visibility:

- *invisible*: the category of gender is not used, leading to gender being invisible;
- *focus on women*: to end the violations of women's human rights and gender-based violence against women;
- *gender mainstreaming*: making gender specificities visible by disaggregating by gender and revising categories to allow gender dimensions to be fully included.

Expressions of each approach are embedded in various laws and policy instruments of the UN, Council of Europe, EU and individual states. These may be understood to represent different legal traditions and instruments: universal human rights, violence against women as a violation of women's human rights and gender-based violence as a form of gender discrimination[99]. They may be understood as based in different schools of feminist theory[100]. They may also be regarded as steps in a developmental trajectory, moving from the understanding that universalism does not provide gender neutrality, to a focus on women, to refining the multidimensional nature of gender relations.

---

[99]   Walby, S. and Olive, P. (2013) *The European Added Value of a Directive on Combatting Violence Against Women: Annex 2 Economic Aspects and Legal Perspectives for Action at the European Level.* Brussels, European Parliament European Value Added Unit.

[100]   Shepherd, L. (2008) *Gender, Violence, Security.* London, Zed.

Invisible gender

Gender has been invisible in many academic and policy fields as well as international law. Gender may also be segregated into an adjacent field that is marginal to the mainstream. There are several reasons why gender may be made invisible. It may be the consequence of neglect of gender, a considered claim that gender is not relevant, or a claim that the absence of gender is a route to gender neutrality. The neglect of gender is the most common of these practices, with little attempt at justification. This has been shown to be mistaken on many occasions[101]. In some cases, the exclusion of gender from core concepts is not a matter of neglect but attempts are made to explicitly justify it. In other instances, the absence of gender has been claimed to be a route to gender justice and the meaning of its absence claimed to be gender neutrality, not gender bias.

In some cases, the invisibility of gender is defended as gender neutrality in aid of universalism. Some human rights texts have been interpreted as if this is their implied approach, including the UN *Universal Declaration of Human Rights*[102] and the *European Convention of Human Rights*[103]. Some international (UN) health-based definitions of violence by the WHO, including in its International Classification of Diseases[104], make no reference to gender in their core components. There is sometimes a deliberate de-gendering of concepts to develop a gender-neutral approach. An example is the de-gendering of the categories of victims and perpetrators in rape law by the extension of the range of pertinent objects and orifices, meaning rape is no longer an offence that only men can commit against only women (see discussion in Chapter Four).

Criticisms of this approach are that it makes invisible relevant aspects of human rights, justice, crime and violence. Further, the claim

[101] Walklate, S. (2001) *Gender, Crime and Criminal Justice*. London, Routledge.
[102] UN (1948) *Op cit*. Footnote 27.
[103] ECtHR (1953) *Op cit*. Footnote 53.
[104] WHO (2014) *International Classification of Diseases (ICD)*. www.who.int/classifications/icd/en/ [November 2016].

to universalism is gender-biased rather than gender-neutral, since categories are often implicitly gendered in a way that is biased towards the dominant gender; as such, 'gender neutral' is actually gendered to the advantage of one sex.

A variant of this approach is to make gender visible in the main area while recognising it as relevant for an adjacent area. The International Classification of Crimes for Statistical Purposes (ICCS) produced by the UNODC does not include gender in its four tiers of classification, but it does include it in its secondary, optional tags[105]. This marginalises gender to 'context' and excludes it from the core concepts on which the classification is built. Gender becomes something about which information is collected on an optional basis, as a secondary tag, not a primary code in the classification.

There have been many challenges to the invisibility of gender. Early challenges focused on including women[106]; later ones sought to include multifaceted dimensions of gender relations[107].

A focus on women

The second approach is to focus on women. Instead of absence, women are made visible. There has been a strong movement to recognise and contest violence against women.

The gender neutrality of the universalism of the UN's *Universal Declaration of Human Rights* was challenged with a demand to explicitly include women's human rights[108]. The UN responded by recognising the specificity of women's human rights, which included the right of

---

[105] UNDOC (2015) *Op cit.* Footnote 33.

[106] Peters, J. and Wolper, A. (1995) *Women's Rights, Human Rights.* New York, Routledge; MacKinnon, C. (2006) *Are Women Human?* Cambridge, MA, Harvard University Press.

[107] Consuelo, C. and Stöckl, H. (2014) 'Intimate partner homicide in 10 European countries: Statistical data and policy development in a cross-national perspective', *European Journal of Criminology,* 11: 601–18; Dobash, R. and Dobash, R. (2004) 'Women's violence to men in intimate relationships: working on a puzzle', *British Journal of Criminology,* 44: 324–49.

[108] Peters, J. and Wolper, A. (1995) *Op cit.* Footnote 106; MacKinnon, C. (2007) *Op cit.* Footnote 106.

women to be free from gender-based violence. A key moment in this development of the international legal regime was recognition of the demand that women's rights be explicitly and not merely implicitly included as human rights[109]. The United Nations 1993 *Declaration on the Elimination of Violence against Women* (DEVAW)[110] defines violence against women as 'any act of gender-based violence that results in, or is likely to result in, physical, sexual or psychological harm or suffering to women, including threats of such acts, coercion or arbitrary deprivation of liberty, whether occurring in public or in private life'. Since this Declaration, the focus on women and on violence against women being a violation of women's human rights has rippled through the UN system. It is embedded in the UN Security Council Resolution 1325 on addressing violence against women in conflict zones[111]. It is adopted in the work of the UN Statistics Commission on indicators on violence against women[112] and their manual on violence against women statistics[113]. A policy focus on 'violence against women' is found in the UNiTE campaign led by the UN Secretary-General[114]. WHO adopts a focus on women in its specialised surveys on violence against women[115].

The focus on women has been in alignment with the development of women's projects to eliminate violence against women, which have helped to construct women as an active political subject in

[109] Kelly, L. (2006) 'Inside outsiders: mainstreaming violence against women into human rights discourse and practice', *International Feminist Journal of Politics*, 7: 471–95.

[110] United Nations General Assembly (1993) *Op cit.* Footnote 30.

[111] UN Security Council (2000) *Resolution on Women, Peace and Security: Security Council Resolution 1325*. https://documents-dds-ny.un.org/doc/UNDOC/GEN/N00/720/18/PDF/N0072018.pdf?OpenElement [November 2016]; Pratt, N. (2011) 'Critically examining UNSCR 1325 on women, peace and security', *International Feminist Journal of Politics*, 13: 489–503.

[112] United Nations Statistical Commission (2010) *Op cit.* Footnote 40.

[113] UN Statistics Commission (2014) *Guidelines for Producing Statistics on Violence against Women*. http://unstats.un.org/unsd/gender/docs/Guidelines_Statistics_VAW.pdf [November 2016].

[114] UN Secretary-General (2016) *UNiTE to End Violence against Women*. http://endviolence.un.org/ [November 2016].

[115] WHO (2005) *Op cit.* Footnote 45.

democratic arenas[116]. 'Violence against women' has also been aligned with a preferred unit of measurement – victims – to ensure that public services to assist those who have suffered the violence remain 'victim-centred'.

Several challenges have been made to framing the issue as 'violence against women'. It omits men who might be subject to violence in gender-saturated contexts, such as domestic violence[117]. The focus on women rather than gender tends to essentialise the categories of women and men[118]. It creates a specialised field that is isolated from the mainstream, where most resources and capacity are located.

Gender mainstreaming

The third approach is gender mainstreaming. This invokes a concept of gender justice that mobilises the concept of gender discrimination, identifies a multiplicity of places where gender inequality is relevant and practices gender disaggregation of mainstream statistics. This approach is found in international, regional and national legal instruments, policies and statistical practices.

Violence against women is a form of gender discrimination in international law. The concept 'discrimination against women' has meaning within the UN system as a consequence of its definition within Article 1[119] of the UN 1979 *Convention on the Elimination of Discrimination against Women* (CEDAW)[120]. CEDAW defines violence

---

[116]   Walby, S. (2011) *The Future of Feminism*. Cambridge, Polity Press; Dobash, R. and Dobash, R. (1992) *Op cit.* Footnote 16.

[117]   Archer, J. (2000) 'Sex differences in aggression between heterosexual partners: a meta-analysis', *Psychological Bulletin*, 126: 651–80.

[118]   Shepherd, L. (2007) 'Victims, perpetrators and actors revisited: exploring the potential for a feminist reconceptualization of (international) security and (gender) violence', *British Journal of Politics and International Relations*, 9: 239–56.

[119]   'For the purposes of the present Convention, the term "discrimination against women" shall mean any distinction, exclusion or restriction made on the basis of sex which has the effect or purpose of impairing or nullifying the recognition, enjoyment or exercise by women, irrespective of their marital status, on a basis of equality of men and women, of human rights and fundamental freedoms in the political, economic, social, cultural, civil or any other field.'

[120]   UN (1979) *Op cit.* Footnote 28.

against women as a form of gender discrimination in General Recommendation 19[121]:

> Gender-based violence is a form of discrimination that seriously inhibits women's ability to enjoy rights and freedoms on a basis of equality with men.

> The definition of discrimination includes gender-based violence, that is, violence that is directed against a woman because she is a woman or that affects women disproportionately.

> Gender-based violence, which impairs or nullifies the enjoyment by women of human rights and fundamental freedoms under general international law or under human rights conventions, is discrimination within the meaning of article 1 of the Convention.

Within the EU, a similar approach to gender equality is embedded in its founding Treaty of Rome on equal pay for women and men and in the current Treaty of Lisbon as equal treatment and non-discrimination. The focus is gender equality rather than women's human rights, although these are not incompatible. The competence of the EU-level to act to implement this principle of gender equality through the legal concept of 'equal treatment' has slowly expanded. Consequent on the Treaty of Lisbon in 2006, there has been an expansion of the competence of the EU-level in the area of 'freedom, security and justice', drawing on Article 82 (and sometimes 83) of the Treaty on the Functioning of the European Union as the basis for Directives on trafficking, child sex abuse, domestic protection orders and victim support.

The implication of the gender mainstreaming approach for data collection is to disaggregate mainstream statistics by gender rather than to develop specialised statistics on women only. For example,

[121]   UN (1992) *Op cit*. Footnote 29.

this entails gender disaggregation of statistics on violence collected in general victimisation surveys[122], rather than specialised surveys concerned only with violence against women.

The approaches of 'focus on women' and 'gender mainstreaming' can sometimes appear as if they were alternatives to each other. However, scrutiny of UN, Council of Europe and EU legal and policy documents finds that they are usually co-present – even in the same sentence. Gender-based violence is both a violation of women's human rights and a form of gender discrimination. In practice, in these international policy documents they are rarely treated as alternatives but rather as mutually reinforcing principles.

This is the approach taken in CEDAW Recommendation 19, which refers to 'the close connection between discrimination against women, gender-based violence, and violations of human rights and fundamental freedoms'[123]. Further examples of this hybrid approach include the UN Beijing Platform for Action[124] and in 2011 the Council of Europe's *Istanbul Convention on Preventing and Combating Violence against Women and Domestic Violence*, which requires Parties to cover not only all forms of violence against women but also domestic violence, which extends (on an optional basis, though they are encouraged to do so) to all victims of domestic violence, including men[125]. This issue becomes more complex when the intersection of gender with other inequalities is taken adequately into account, since making gender visible has implications for the visibility of intersecting inequalities[126].

The inclusion of a gender dimension requires more than the introduction of the category of gender into policy; it requires the revision of mainstream concepts and practices. In a policy context,

---

[122] Walby, S., Towers, J. and Francis, B. (2014) *Op cit.* Footnote 90; Walby, S., Towers, J. and Francis, B. (2016) *Op cit.* Footnote 6.

[123] UN (1992) *CEDAW*, Recommendation 19, point 4. www.un.org/womenwatch/daw/cedaw/recommendations/recomm.htm#top [November 2016].

[124] UN (1995) *Op cit.* Footnote 31.

[125] Council of Europe (2011) *Op cit.* Footnote 47.

[126] Crenshaw, K. (1991) 'Mapping the margins: intersectionality, identity politics and violence against women of colour', *Stanford Law Review*, 43: 1241–99; Walby, S., Strid, S. and Armstrong, J. (2012) 'Intersectionality and the quality of the gender equality architecture', *Social Politics*, 19: 446–81.

this means addressing the activities of all policy actors, not only those that are focused on women.

Gender mainstreaming was institutionalised as an approach to gender equality issues, including violence against women, in the UN 1995 Beijing Platform for Action[127]. At paragraph 123 it states: 'In addressing violence against women, Governments and other actors should promote an active and visible policy of mainstreaming a gender perspective in all policies and programmes so that before decisions are taken an analysis may be made of their effects on women and men, respectively.' The European Commission defined gender mainstreaming thus in 1996:

Gender mainstreaming involves not restricting efforts to promote equality to the implementation of specific measures to help women, but mobilising all general policies and measures specifically for the purpose of achieving equality by actively and openly taking into account at the planning stage their possible effects on the respective situation of men and women (gender perspective). This means systematically examining measures and policies and taking into account such possible effects when defining and implementing them[128].

Similarly, the Council of Europe describes gender mainstreaming as: 'The (re)organization, improvement, development and evaluation of policy processes, so that a gender equality perspective is incorporated in all policies, at all levels'[129].

---

[127] UN (1995) *Op cit.* Footnote 31.
[128] EC (1996) *Incorporating Equal Opportunities for Women and Men into all Community Policies and Activities*, COM(1996) 67 final. http://aei.pitt.edu/3991/ [November 2016].
[129] Council of Europe (1998) *Gender Mainstreaming: Conceptual Framework, Methodology and Presentation of Good Practices*. Strasbourg, Council of Europe.

The inclusion of the gender equality perspective in the mainstream is a challenge[130]. There is a dilemma as to the extent to which gender issues are better addressed separately and the extent to which they are better addressed within the wider system. The advantage of separate development is that specialist and expert knowledge can be more easily developed, while the disadvantage is that the knowledge developed is regarded as relevant only to that specialism, so it becomes isolated and with few resources. The advantage of being inside the mainstream is the possibility of accessing resources for development, while the risk is that a series of compromises dilutes or removes key elements, so that the gender equality perspective is merely absorbed by the mainstream rather than changing it.

There is no easy or permanent resolution to this tension between mainstream and specialised perspectives. The best approach is to treat this tension as a source of dynamism that is productive to both the agenda of gender equality and the improved performance of the mainstream on its own terms[131]. This entails an approach of developing specialist expertise and knowledge *and* simultaneously engaging with reform of mainstream structures of knowledge.

For statistical purposes, the best way forward is to provide data that is gender disaggregated and includes all relevant categories, since this would support the conceptualisation of gender-based violence as both a violation of women's human rights and a form of gender discrimination.

Dimensions of gender

Taking gender seriously means identifying the sex of the victim and perpetrator and identifying further gender saturated dimensions. Identifying the sex of victim and of the perpetrator is important but not sufficient. Gendering statistics means more than adding gender

---

[130]   Walby, S. (2005) 'Gender mainstreaming: productive tensions in theory and practice', *Social Politics*, 12: 321–43; Daly, M. (2005) 'Gender mainstreaming in theory and practice', *Social Politics*, 12: 433–50.

[131]   Walby, S. (2005) *Op cit.* Footnote 130.

as a variable[132]; more than the gender disaggregation of existing data on victims and perpetrators. It entails the inclusion of information about several gender-saturated dimensions of the violence that is core to the definition of the event. In the context of violence, this especially concerns domestic and sexual relations. It should include the recognition of transgender and pangender. Gender-saturated dimensions include domestic relationships (intimate partnerships or other family members) (as compared to acquaintances and strangers), whether there was a sexual aspect and (potentially) gender motivation. Gender 'saturates' because gender inflects or shapes practice but is not the sole determinant.

Four gender dimensions are required, while a fifth and further dimension may sometimes apply:

1. The sex of the victim.
2. The sex of the perpetrator.
3. The relationship between perpetrator and victim: whether the perpetrator was a domestic relation, either (current or former) intimate partner of the victim or another family member (either blood relative or other household member), an acquaintance or a stranger.
4. Whether there was a sexual aspect to the violence as well as physical.
5. In some events it is possible to discern a gender motivation.

Further types of gender-saturated contexts can also be relevant in some situations.

First, the sex of the victim is essential in order to measure 'violence against women' and to gender disaggregate statistics on violence.

Second, the sex of the perpetrator is important in order to ascertain the extent and nature of gender-based violence.

A third important gender-saturated dimension is the 'domestic'. In the context of violence, this means identifying whether there is a domestic relationship between the perpetrator and victim. A domestic

---

[132]   Johnson, H. (2015) *Op cit*. Footnote 23.

relationship can take one of two main forms: intimate partner and other family members. Forms of differentiation concerning intimates are between current and former intimate partners and between spouses, partners and boyfriends/girlfriends. Forms of differentiation for family members are between blood relatives and other family members.

The UNODC ICCS[133] usefully distinguishes between 11 types of perpetrator–victim relationships: current intimate partner/spouse; former intimate partner/spouse; blood relative; other household member; friend; acquaintance; colleague/work relationship; authority/ care relationship (doctor, nurse, police and so on); other offender known to victim, offender unknown to victim and relationship not known. These are similar (but not identical) to the disaggregations the UNODC ICCS[134] lists as additional disaggregations for intentional homicide, which offer a more structured disaggregation: intimate partner or family member (IPFM), other perpetrator known to the victim and perpetrator unknown to the victim. Intimate partners are further disaggregated into: current spouse; current cohabiting partner; current non-cohabiting partner (boyfriend/girlfriend but not married); former spouse, former cohabiting partner and former non-cohabiting partner (boyfriend/girlfriend but not married). Family members are further disaggregated into blood relatives and other household members (living in the same household as the victim) and relative by marriage or adoption. Blood relatives are further disaggregated into parent, child, cohabiting blood relative and non-cohabiting blood relative. Other perpetrators known to the victim are disaggregated by: friend or acquaintance (separately identified); colleague/business or work relationship, authority/care relationship and other perpetrator known to victim. These are useful distinctions. They contain information about not only domestic relations but also positions of authority. However, it is regretful that the UNODC ICCS lists for perpetrator–victim relationships are slightly different for crimes other

133 UNODC (2015) *Op cit:* 100-1. Footnote 33.
134 UNODC (2015) *Op cit:* 103. Footnote 33.

than homicide from those for intentional homicide. One or the other should become the preferred list.

A fourth gender-saturated dimension is the sexual aspect. This overlaps with the domestic category of intimate partner but is wider, since it includes non-consensual sex from non-partners. It is relevant to sexual offences (rape and other sexual assaults) in understanding them as gendered – whether they entail heterosexual or lesbian, gay, bisexual, queer, transgender and intersex (LGBQTI) relations. It is relevant to rape–murder and its inclusion within the category of femicide. It is relevant to FGM.

A fifth potential gender-saturated dimension is motivation. This is much more difficult for data collection (and legal adjudication), since it is not usually easily observable. In some instances, this may be useful but not essential extra data for specific local purposes. For example, in the case of a domestic homicide motivated by dowry issues, the additional information about the dowry motivation is useful but not necessary to determine whether or not the death was a domestic homicide. Coercive control is a further example; this is addressed later, since it also pertains to the issue of the boundary between violence and not-violence.

Further gender-saturated dimensions are relevant in some instances. One of these is 'location' or 'setting'. In some services (such as health), information is more often collected on the location of the violence than on the perpetrator–victim relationship; however, 'location' may be a proxy that in practice approximates 'relationship'. For example, there is a likelihood that violence in a 'domestic location' is perpetrated by a domestic relation, though this is not always the case. Where information on relationship is not collected, information on location is significant.

Conclusions on the concept of gender

It is important to revise the mainstream measurement frameworks and indicators, not only the specialist ones. The majority of well-resourced data collection occurs during the administration of major public services (such as police, courts and health) and in the most repeated population surveys (such as crime and health). It is important to ensure that the new categories essential for the understanding of violence against women and gender-based violence are included in mainstream frameworks, so that gender is not reduced to being merely a variable for existing categories[135]. It is not enough to have disaggregation by gender; it is also important to ensure that gender-saturated concepts are operationalised and included in the official measurement framework.

It is necessary to achieve not only the gender disaggregation of traditional categories but also the inclusion of the categories necessary to understand gender-based violence. This means rejecting the stance of gender neutrality while recognising that this can sometimes be a well-intentioned strategy. The practice of de-gendering a previously gendered approach is not justified. Making something invisible is not a route to understanding or justice that is likely to be successful. It means rejecting collecting data on women only while recognising the merits of affording special attention to women and the importance of building specific sites of expertise. It is necessary to engage with mainstream systems of knowledge and providers of services.

This has implications for the indicators that summarise complex statistical information on violence. It is necessary to change the indicators, introducing new ones as well as disaggregating the traditional ones. This means including the sex of the victim and perpetrator, the relationship between perpetrator and victim, whether violence has a sexual aspect and when it is gender motivated.

[135] Johnson, H. (2015) *Op cit.* Footnote 23.

4

DIFFERENT FORMS
OF VIOLENCE

Introduction

There are different forms of violence against women and men. These differences in forms potentially have implications for their measurement. This chapter addresses the nuances required for the measurement framework to take these differences into account, although it is important not to overstate the differences.

The typology of forms of violence proposed here is based in international legal instruments, as discussed in Chapter Two. These include the UN *Declaration on the Elimination of Violence against Women* (DEVAW) [136] and the UN *Convention on the Elimination of Discrimination against Women* (CEDAW)[137]. There is attention to the regional Conventions on gender-based violence, including the Council of Europe *Istanbul Convention on Preventing and Combating Violence against Women and Domestic Violence*[138] and the *Inter-American Convention on the Prevention, Punishment and Eradication of Violence against Women, 'Convention of Belem do Para'*[139].

---

[136] UN General Assembly (1993) *Op cit*. Footnote 30.
[137] UN (1979) *Op cit*. Footnote 28.
[138] Council of Europe (2011) *Op cit*. Footnote 47.
[139] Organisation of American States (1994) *Op cit*. Footnote 48.

While this book focuses on violence, the boundary between violence and non-physical coercion is often unclear, so both are – at least initially – included in the framework in order that they can be measured in relation to each other. Coercion may take non-violent forms but could also include physical force; hence, it straddles the violence/not-violence boundary.

Specific forms of violence or coercion are addressed in this chapter, which affords most attention to homicide/femicide; assault; sexual violence including rape; and female genital mutilation (FGM). The chapter addresses definition, measurement unit, data collection and implications for measurement. It also discusses the categories of 'domestic violence' and 'violence against women'.

Physical violence: homicide/femicide

Introduction

Physical violence is a distinctive form of violence. This section discusses homicide/femicide and assault.

Definition

Homicide is the illegal killing of women and men.

While the main contours of homicide might appear clear, there are nonetheless issues concerning the boundary of the concept. These include the boundary between legal and illegal killings; the continuum of intentionality; violence oriented to one's own body; age limits and the exclusion of children; and whether data initially recorded is revised as better information becomes available. While these issues can be relevant to other forms of violence, they are particularly sharply drawn in the case of killing.

Illegal killings: Killing by soldiers acting under orders in war and killing in self-defence are usually excluded from homicide, though they would be relevant if legal violence were to be included. However, international law on war crimes means that not all actions in war are legal. Further, the boundary between illegal and legal can be hard to determine in practice in conflict zones.

Intent: Gradations in intent to kill are relevant in determining the type of homicide. There are gradations in intent that differentiate homicide, murder, manslaughter and death due to reckless behaviour leading to unintentional homicide (such as death by dangerous driving). This gradation may be gendered in cases of domestic homicide, where the use of violence in 'the heat of the moment' tends to be treated more leniently than violence used in a premeditated act, even if it was a defensive response to prior violence.

Crimes related to a person's own body: Issues here include illegal abortion and assisted suicide, the legality of which varies between countries.

Consistent dates and location of recording: While these technical issues are relevant to all violent crime, they are often more sharply drawn in the case of homicide. The date of homicide may be the date of its discovery or the estimated date of death. The location may be where the killing took place or where the body was found. A record may be permanent or subject to revision as better information comes to light; for example, the removal of cases that investigation reveals to be natural deaths, or those that are later proven in court not to be homicides, or where the victim dies later. There are also differences as to whether only completed or both attempted and completed homicides are included.

Issues concerning the gender dimensions include the sex of the victim; the sex of the perpetrator; the gender-saturated context of an intimate partner or other family member; where there is a sexual aspect; and gendered motivation.

These gender dimensions are associated with different approaches to gender and homicide: the killing of women and girls regardless of motive or perpetrator status; the killing of women in gender-saturated contexts, especially but not only by male intimate partners; and the intentionally misogynist killing of women and girls by men, in association with patriarchy. There is much debate over the meaning of the term 'femicide' and whether it applies to all or only some of these types of killing. The term femicide[140] challenges the gender neutrality of the concept of homicide. Whether the term should be defined broadly or narrowly is much debated: is it the homicide of any woman, or is it restricted to the killing of women in gender-saturated contexts or when there is a gendered motivation[141]?

[140] Introduced by Russell during the proceedings of the First International Tribunal on Crimes against Women in 1976 (Radford, J. and Russell, D. (1992) *Femicide: The Politics of Woman Killing.* Woodbridge, Twayne Publishing: xiv).

[141] Recent discussions include: the UN (2013) General Assembly Resolution (68/191) on taking action against gender-related killing of women and girls; contributions to the UNODC/UN Statistical Division SD (2015) event at the Commission on the Status of Women; the WHO (2012) report WHO/RHR/12.38; the UN 2012 Symposium on Femicide, the *Handbook on European Homicide Research* and the EU COST Network on Femicide. UN General Assembly (2013) *Resolution 68/191 (A/RES/68/191) Taking Action against gender Related Killings of Women and Girls.* www.unodc.org/documents/commissions/CCPCJ/Crime_ Resolutions/2010-2019/2013/General_Assembly/A-RES-68-191.pdf [November 2016]; UNODC/UNSD (2015) *Data and Information on Violence against Women to Target Effective Policies.* Side Event to the 59th Session of the Commission on the Status of Women, Italy, UNODC United Nations Statistics Division (UNSD) New York, 16 March. Conference Agenda. http://esango.un.org/SideEvents/ documents/985 [November 2016]; WHO (2012) *Understanding and Addressing Violence against Women: Femicide.* Geneva, World Health Organisation; Russell, D. (2012) *Defining Femicide.* Speech given at the UN Symposium on Femicide: A Global Issue that Demands Action, Vienna, November 2012. www. dianarussell.com/defining-femicide-.html [November 2016]; Francis, B. and Soothill, K. (2012) 'Homicide in England and Wales', in Liem, M. & Pridemore, W. (eds) *Handbook of European Homicide Research: Patterns, Explanations, and Country Studies.* Berlin, Springer: 287–300; Corradi, C. and Stöckl, H. (2014) 'Intimate partner homicide in 10 European countries: statistical data and policy development in a cross-national perspective', *European Journal of Criminology,* 11(5): 601–18; Corradi, C. (2014) '*Il femminicidio in Italia: dimensioni del fenomeno e confronti internazionali* [Femicide in Italy: national characteristics and international comparisons]' in Cimagalli, F. (ed.) *Politiche contro la violenza di genere nel welfare che cambia.* Milan, Franco Angeli: 157–69; Weil, S. (2014) *What is Femicide? Concepts and Definitions.* Proceedings of Working Group 1 on Definitions, COST Action IS 1206 Femicide across Europe, Jerusalem, The Hebrew University of Jerusalem, 24 October; Consuelo, C., Marcuello-Servos, C., Boira, S. and Weil, S. (2015) 'Theories of femicide and their significance for social research', *Current Sociology.* Epub ahead of print, January 2016. DOI: 10.1177/0011392115622256.

Sex of the victim

When the victim of homicide is female, the term female homicide is used more often than that of femicide in mainstream criminology[142].
Others use the term femicide to refer to the same concept of the homicide of women[143]. For example, for Campbell and Runyan, femicide 'refers to all killings of women, regardless of motive or perpetrator status'[144].
The United Nations Office on Drugs and Crime (UNODC) International Classification of Crimes for Statistical Purposes (ICCS)[145] does not include the sex of the victim within its mandatory coding scheme for homicide; it is only included as an optional 'tag'.

[142] Pridemore, W. and Freilich, J (2005) 'Gender equality, traditional masculine culture and female homicide victimisation', *Journal of Criminal Justice*, 33: 213–23; Titterington, V. (2006) 'A retrospective investigation of gender inequality and female homicide victimisation', *Sociological Spectrum*, 26: 205–6; Stamatel, J. (2014) 'Explaining variations in female homicide victimisation rates across Europe', *European Journal of Criminology*, 11: 578–600.

[143] Mouzos, J. (1999) 'Femicide: an overview of major findings', *Australian Institute of Criminology: Trends and Issues in Crime and Criminal Justice*, 124: 1–6; Campbell, J., Webster, D., Koziol-McLain, J., Block, C., Campbell, D., Curry, M., Gary, F., Glass, N., McFarlane, J., Sachs, C., Sharp, P., Ulrich, Y., Wilt, S., Manganello, J., Xu, X., Schollenberger, J., Frye, V. and Laughon, K. (2003) 'Risk factors for femicide in abusive relationships', *American Journal of Public Health*, 93(7): 1089–97; Lezzi, D. (2010) 'Intimate femicide in Italy: a model to classify how killings happened', in Palumbo, F., Lauro, C. and Greenacre, M. (eds) *Data Analysis and Classification*. Berlin, Springer-Verlag: 85–91; Muftic, L. and Bauman, M. (2012) 'Female versus male perpetrated femicide: an exploratory analysis of whether offender gender matters', *Journal of Interpersonal Violence*, 27: 2824–44; Bonanni, E., Maiese, A., Gitto, L., Falco, P., Maiese, A. and Bolino, G. (2014) 'Femicide in Italy: national scenario and presentation of four cases', *Medico–Legal Journal*, 82: 32–7; Corradi, C. (2014) '*Il femminicidio in Italia: dimensioni del fenomeno e confronti internazionali* [Femicide in Italy: characteristics and international comparisons]', in Cimagalli, F. (ed) *Politiche contro la Violenza di Genere nel Welfare che Cambia*. Milan, Franco Angeli: 157–69.

[144] Campbell, J. and Runyan, C. (1998) 'Femicide: guest editors introduction', *Homicide Studies*, 2(4): 347–52.

[145] UNODC (2015) *Op cit*: 33, 100. Footnote 33.

Sex of the perpetrator

The sex of the perpetrator is relevant to the analysis of the gender dimensions of violence. In particular, discussions of femicide often focus on killings where the perpetrator is male and the victim is female. Little data is systematically presented on the sex of the perpetrator, even though this information is almost always recorded somewhere in administrative systems where there is a suspected or proven perpetrator.

The UNODC ICCS[146] includes the sex of the perpetrator only as an optional tag; it is not a mandatory code.

Relationship between perpetrator and victim

Intimate partners are the most frequent perpetrators of the homicide of women[147]. Some use the term 'intimate partner homicide' for this violence, implying that this is a subset of the more general field of homicide studies[148]. Others use the term 'intimate partner femicide'

---

[146]   UNODC (2015) *Op cit.* Footnote 33.

[147]   Caputi, J. and Russell, D. (1992) 'Femicide: sexist terrorism against women', in Radford, J. and Russell, D. (eds) *Femicide.* Cengage Gale, Farmington Hills: 13–21; Campbell, J. (1992) '"If I can't have you no one can": power and control in homicide of female partners', in Radford, J. and Russell, D. (eds) *Femicide.* Cengage Gale, Farmington Hills: 99–113; Wilson, M. and Daly, M. (1992) 'Till death do us part', in Radford, J. and Russell, D. (eds) *Femicide.* Cengage Gale, Farmington Hills: 83–98.

[148]   Dugan, I., Nagin, D and Rosenfeld, R. (2003) 'Exposure reduction or retaliation? The effects of domestic violence resources on intimate partner homicide', *Law & Society Review,* 37: 169–98; Campbell, J., Glass, N., Sharps, P., Laughon, K. and Bloom, T. (2007) 'Intimate partner homicide: review and implications for research and policy', *Trauma, Violence and Abuse,* 8: 246–69; Stöckl, H., Devries, K., Rotstein, A., Abrahams, N., Campbell, J., Watts, C. and Garcia Moreno, C. (2013) 'The global prevalence of intimate partner homicide: a systematic review', *The Lancet,* 382: 859–65; Corradi, C. and Stöckl, H. (2014) *Op cit.* Footnote 141.

for the same type of violence[149], while others attempt to merge the two approaches; for example, Stout[150] defines femicide as the killing of women by male intimate partners without special reference to misogyny, maintaining that 'there is no single cause of homicide, violence against women, or intimate femicide' and suggesting an ecological framework that allows 'the opportunity to merge feminist world views with more traditional models on homicide'[151].

The UNODC ICCS[152] recommends optional tags, not mandatory codes, for the relationships between perpetrator and victim in the case of homicide (these were listed in Chapter Three).

Sex–murder

A homicide may be gender saturated if it takes place in the context of sexual assault. A sexual murder occurs if there is evidence of sexual assault; rape; mutilation of the sexual areas of the victim' body; masturbation over the body; an absence of clothing; or an arrangement of clothing that indicates a sexual motive[153].

The UNODC ICCS[154] recognises sexual assault as an additional disaggregation of intentional homicide in relation to the mechanism of the killing, but sexual assault is only recognised within the category of 'force'. The legal boundary to sexual assault is 'consent', not 'force'. In addition, this distinction is merely an optional tag, not a mandatory code, and is thus highly problematic.

[149] Frye, V., Sandro, G., Tray, M., Bucciarelli, A., Putnam, S. and Wilt, S. (2008) 'The role of neighbourhood environment and risk of intimate partner femicide in a large urban area', *American Journal of Public Health*, 98: 1473–9; Dixon, L., Hamilton-Giachritsis, C. and Brown, K. (2008) 'Classifying intimate partner femicide 2008', *Journal of Intimate Partner Violence*, 23: 74–93; Taylor, R. and Jasinski, J. (2011) 'Femicide and the feminist perspective', *Homicide Studies*, 15: 341–62.
[150] Stout, K. (1992) 'Intimate femicide: an ecological analysis', *Journal of Sociology and Social Welfare*, 29: 29–50.
[151] Stout, K. (1992) *Op cit:* 30. Footnote 150.
[152] UNODC (2015) *Op cit:* 103. Footnote 33.
[153] Dobash, R. and Dobash, R. (2015) *When Men Murder Women*. Oxford, Oxford University Press.
[154] UNODC (2015) *Op cit:* 104. Footnote 33.

Gender motivation

'Intentional', when applied to violent crime, typically means that the victim was targeted by the perpetrator either in the heat of the moment or as a result of some degree of planning and/or that the perpetrator desires the consequences of their act or acquiesces to these consequences[155]. In the context of femicide, there can be a more narrowly targeted meaning[156]. Radford defines femicide as 'the misogynous killing of women by men', motivated by hatred, contempt, pleasure or a sense of ownership of women and thus to be investigated 'in the context of the overall oppression of women in a patriarchal society'[157]. She extends femicide to many different forms: racist femicide; lesbicide; deliberate transmission of HIV virus by rapist; death resulting from botched abortion, infanticide and deaths of baby girls from neglect and starvation[158]. The Academic Council of the United Nations (ACUNS) also distinguishes between forms of femicide including murder, honour killing, dowry-related killing, infanticide and gender-based prenatal selection[159].

The UNODC ICCS[160] lists several motivations for homicide under its description of intentional homicide, including 'honour killing', 'dowry-related killings' and 'femicide', which may be regarded as forms of gender-motivated homicide. However, these are neither separately distinguished within its coding scheme nor even in its secondary tag options, despite the referencing of UN documents as authoritative sources of definitions. The UNODC ICCS[161] further

---

[155]   Smit, P., Rinke, R. and Bijleveld, C. (2013) 'Homicide data in Europe: definitions, sources and statistics', in Marieke, L. and Pridemore, W. (eds) *Handbook of European Homicide Research.* New York, Springer: 5.

[156]   Radford, J. and Russell, D. (1992) *Femicide.* Cengage Gale, Farmington Hills; Stout, K. (1992) *Op cit.* Footnote 150.

[157]   Radford, J. and Russell, D. (1992) *Op cit:* 3. Footnote 156.

[158]   Radford, J. and Russell, D. (1992) *Op cit:* 7. Footnote 156.

[159]   Domazetoska, S., Platzer, M. and Plaku, G (eds) (2014) *Femicide: A Global Issue that Demands Action.* Volume 2. Vienna, ACUNS; Laurent, C., Platzer, M. and Idomire, M. (2013) *Femicide.* Volume 1. Vienna, ACUNS; Filip, A. and Platzer, M. (eds) (2015) *Femicide: Targeting Women in Conflict.* Volume 3. Vienna, ACUNS.

[160]   UNODC (2015) *Op cit:* 33. Footnote 33.

[161]   UNODC (2015) *Op cit:* 102. Footnote 33.

notes the significance of the situational context of intentional homicide, including the possibility of sociopolitical homicide motivated by social prejudice concerning sex and gender, but also proposes this merely as an optional 'tag' rather than a mandatory code.

Units of measurement

The units of measurement should include event, victim and perpetrator.

Data collection and coordination

Homicide is the form of violence on which official statistics are more robust than any other. It is recorded by administrative authorities, including the police and health services. Homicide is the only type of violence for which data from administrative records is close to the real level of violence. Surveys are obviously not the main source of data, since surveys usually interview victims. The exception is in conflict zones, where those still alive can be surveyed to ask how many of the people they knew – as family members, neighbours and friends – died as a consequence of the conflict.

Sources of data

The main sources of data are national criminal justice systems, including police, courts and national health systems, though there are additional mechanisms including coroners' courts or mortuaries. These data are available at national, European and international levels. Global datasets on homicide are available from the UNODC[162] and World Health Organization (WHO)[163]. However, producing data on homicide that is exactly comparable is still challenging[164] – though

---

[162] UNODC. *Global Homicide Statistics*. https://data.humdata.org/dataset/unodc-global-homicide-statistics [November 2016].

[163] WHO. *Mortality Data Set*. www.who.int/healthinfo/mortality_data/en/ [November 2016].

[164] Smit et al. (2013) *Op cit*. Footnote 155.

there are initiatives, such as the European Homicide Monitor, to address this[165].

Police records are the source of the majority of national statistics on homicide. Across Europe, police statistics differ in whether they report on suspected or only on convicted perpetrators[166]. In addition, crime statistics might only report the victim–offender relationship in respect to perpetrators of homicides and not victims of homicide, which can be problematic in cases of multiple victims. Some might include attempted homicides; others, only completed homicides.

Court data is based on sentenced homicide perpetrators. Some countries, including the UK, update their national statistics based on police reports with court data[167]. Court records allow better establishment of the motive of the crime – but are limited to those cases that end in court convictions, missing those where evidence was missing or flawed or where the killer committed suicide (homicide–suicides are associated with intimate partner homicides[168]) – and have more information about the perpetrator than the victim. Court data is also time-consuming to examine[169].

Health systems record homicide through the WHO classification system, the International Classification of Diseases (ICD-10). The UNODC suggests that the relevant codes (ICD-10 X85 to Y09: injuries inflicted by another person with intent to injure or kill) are

[165] Ganpat, S., Granath, S., Hagstedt, J., Kivivuori, J., Lehti, M., Liem, M. and Nieuwbeerta, P. (2011) *Homicide in Finland, the Netherlands and Sweden: A First Study on the European Homicide Monitor Data*. Stockholm, The Swedish Council for Crime Prevention.

[166] Smit et al., (2013) *Op cit.* Footnote 155.

[167] Smith, K., Osborne, S., Lau, I. and Briton, A. (2012) *Homicides, Firearm Offences and Intimate Violence 2010/11: Supplementary Volume 2 to Crime in England and Wales*. London, Home Office.

[168] Large, M., Smith, G. and Nielssen, O. (2009) 'The epidemiology of homicide followed by suicide: a systematic and quantitative review', *Suicide and Life Threatening Behavior*, 39: 294–306.

[169] Podreka, J. (2014) 'Intimate partner homicides in Slovenia and their gender-specific differences', *Journal of Criminal Investigation and Criminology/Ljubljana*, 65: 60–73.

'generally corresponding to the definition of intentional homicide'[170], although the data are not identical.

Homicide data is published in a form disaggregated by the sex of the victim in most countries around the world, from the UNODC and WHO as well as national sources. It is further disaggregated by whether the perpetrator is an intimate partner or domestic relation in some countries, including around half of EU Member States, although there are some variations in the definition of 'intimate partner' and 'domestic'. Very few countries publish data on sexual homicides. Very few publish data on the motive of the killing, including gendered motivation. Data on the age of the victim is often published. Some countries produce detailed reviews of domestic homicide cases in order to learn how to improve official responses. However, in some countries the data collected is little more than that which can be derived from the dead body. Data on intimate partner homicide may be collected using different definitions of intimate partners, including spouses, cohabitees, former as well as current partners and same-sex partners[171]. Even when the data is normally collected, there may be gaps[172]; indeed, an average of 20% of missing data has been found in this regard[173], though there are practices to minimise this[174].

Considerably more data is collected than is published. The various agencies that deal with homicide usually have more detailed internal administrative records, but these might only be available in print, in the

---

[170]   UNODC (2013) *Op cit.* Footnote 1.

[171]   Smith et al., (2012) *Op cit.* Footnote 167.

[172]   Quinet, K. and Nunn, S. (2014) 'Establishing the victim-offender relationship of initially unsolved homicides: partner, family, acquaintance, or stranger?' *Homicide Studies*, 18: 271–97; Regoeczi, W. and Riedel, M. (2003) 'The application of missing data estimation models to the problem of unknown victim/offender relationships in homicide cases', *Journal of Quantitative Criminology*, 19: 155–83.

[173]   Stöckl, H. et al., (2013) *Op cit.* Footnote 148.

[174]   Kivivuori, J. and Lehti, M. (2012) 'Social correlates of intimate partner homicide in Finland District or shared with other homicide types', *Homicide Studies*, 16: 60–77; Lehti, M., Kääriäinen, J. and Kivivuori, J. (2012) 'The declining number of child homicides in Finland, 1960–2009', *Homicide Studies*, 16: 3–22; A good example to improve national statistics on the victim offender relationship is Finland, where a police investigation file cannot be closed if all fields in the electronic form are not filled.

local language or on request[175]. Data may not always be representative for the whole country; for example, it may be collected regionally or by local police stations, courts or mortuaries[176]. This may be due to a lack of interest, weak or outdated reporting systems or a lack of cooperation between institutions collecting the data.

There is an emerging field of research on femicide[177] and a developing literature on lethal intimate partner violence[178]; women homicide offending[179]; women victims of lethal violence[180], women dying from intimate partner violence[181] and fatal intimate partner violence[182]. Femicide can also be associated with non-lethal forms of violence, such as battering and assault, occurring prior to femicide[183]. Empirical studies in Europe indicate that femicide happens mainly in intimate partnerships and domestic/family relationships[184]. The majority (65–70%) of intimate partner femicides in the USA have

---

[175] Corraldi, C. and Stöckl, H. (2014) *Op cit.* Footnote 141.

[176] Stöckl, H. et al. (2013) *Op cit.* Footnote 148; Leth, P. (2009) 'Intimate partner homicide', *Forensic Science, Medicine and Pathology*, 5: 199–203.

[177] Femicide research is active in Australia, Canada, Central and South America, South Africa and the US (Path, E. (2009) *Strengthening Understanding of Femicide, Using Research to Galvanise Action and Accountability Meeting*, Washington DC, April 2008) as well as in Europe (Weil, S. (2014) 'What is Femicide? Concepts and definitions'. *Proceedings of Working Group 1 on Definitions, COST Action IS 1206 Femicide Across Europe*. Jerusalem, The Hebrew University of Jerusalem, 24 October 2013).

[178] Dobash, R. and Dobash, R. (2011) 'What were they thinking? Men who murder an intimate partner', *Violence against Women*, 17(1): 111–34.

[179] Dewees, M. and Parker, K. (2003) 'Women, region and type of homicide: are there regional differences in the structural status of women and homicide offending?' *Homicide Studies*, 7: 368–93.

[180] Dobash, R., Dobash, R., Cavanagh, K. and Juanjo, M. (2007) 'Lethal and nonlethal violence against an intimate female partner: comparing male murders to nonlethal abusers', *Violence against Women*, 13: 329–53.

[181] Abrahams, N., Jewkes, R., Martin, L., Matthews, S., Vetten, L. and Lombard, C. (2009) 'Mortality of women from intimate partner violence in South Africa', *Violence and Victims*, 24: 546–56.

[182] Pereira, A., Duarte, N. and Magalhaes, T. (2013) 'Fatal intimate partner violence against women in Portugal: a forensic medical national study', *Journal of Forensic and Legal Medicine*, 20: 1099–107.

[183] Dobash, R. and Dobash, R. (2015) *Op cit.* Footnote 153.

[184] Leth, P. (2009) *Op cit.* Footnote 176; Haller, B. (2014) 'Intimate partner killing: convictions in Australia from 2008 to 2010', *SWS-Rundschau*, 54: 59–77; Stöckl, H. et al. (2013) *Op cit.* Footnote 148.

been shown to be preceded by partner violence[185]. There are studies that address multiple levels of causation[186]. Another approach consists of taking detailed analyses of female homicides from different sources, such as police and court files, mortuary data and newspaper reports[187].

Implications for measurement

Despite difficulties in producing data that is exactly comparable between countries, homicide data is the most robust measure of violence. Among all forms of violence, homicide has the most developed data collection on the five gender dimensions. It is currently globally available disaggregated by the sex of the victim; however, there is significant variation in the extent to which data on the further four dimensions are collected and/or presented. Further development of data collection and presentation using comparable definitions and the remaining gender dimensions is needed.

Homicide – disaggregated by the five gender dimensions, starting with the sex of the victim – is the best candidate for an indicator of changes in violence over time and comparing countries.

---

[185]   Campbell, J. et al. (2007) *Op cit:* 247. Footnote 148.

[186]   Stout, K. (1992) *Op cit.* Footnote 150; Dugan, L. et al. (2003) *Op cit.* Footnote 148; Muftic, L. and Baumann, M. (2012) *Op cit.* Footnote 143; Stamatel, J. (2014) *Op cit.* Footnote 142.

[187]   Ministere de l'Interieur (2011) *'Etude nationale sur les morts violentes au sein du couple: Annee 2010'* ('National study on violent deaths in couples: 2010'), Ministere de l'Interieur: Delegation aux victims, Diection Generale de la police nationale, Direction generale de la gendarmerie nationale; Ministerio de Sanidad Servicios Sociales e Igualdad (2013) *5th Annual Report by the National Observatory on Violence against Women 2012.* Madrid, Ministerio de Sanidad, Servicios Sociales e Igualdad; Bugeja, L., Butler, A., Buxton, A., Buxton, E., Ehrat, H., Hayes, M., McIntyre, S. and Walsh, C. (2013) 'The implementation of domestic violence death reviews in Australia', *Homicide Studies,* 17: 353–74.

Physical violence: assault

Introduction

Assault is non-lethal physical violence. A distinctive set of measurement challenges concern the boundary between assault and not-violence when there are few or no physical injuries. In most respects, the measurement issues are similar to those of homicide, except that administrative data is not an accurate measure of the extent of physical assaults since only a minority of these is reported to administrative bodies such as police or health services.

Definition

In some countries, assault that does not lead to visible injury is not treated as a violent crime. Hence, the definition of assault requires clarity and harmonisation. The *Istanbul Convention* does not make distinctions within the category of physical violence. The UNODC ICCS[188] distinguishes two levels of assault: serious assault – 'intentional or reckless application of serious physical force inflicted upon the body of a person resulting in serious bodily injury' (020111) – and minor physical force – 'no injury or minor bodily injury' (020112).

The potential gender dimensions of assault are the same as for other forms of violence: sex of victim; sex of perpetrator; relationship between perpetrator and victim; sexual aspect; and gender motivation.

It is important to include a category of assault separately from that of domestic violence (discussed later). Indeed much assault against women is perpetrated by acquaintances and some by strangers, as are many assaults against men[189].

---

[188] UNODC (2015) *Op cit:* 37. Footnote 33.
[189] Walby, S., Towers, J. and Francis, B. (2014) *Op cit.* Footnote 90.

Implications for measurement

All assaults should be included in the measurement framework, whether or not they caused visible physical injury. All three measurement units are important: event, victim and perpetrator. Unlike homicide, the majority of assaults are not reported to the authorities, so administrative statistics will not deliver an accurate picture of the extent of this form of violence. Surveys are thus important means of generating data. In victim-focused surveys, attention needs to be paid to ensuring the full counting of events and perpetrators as well as victims.

Sexual violence, including rape

Introduction

Sexual violence is a specific form of violence concerning contact with the body in the absence of consent that violates sexual autonomy. Rape is a subset of sexual violence that includes penetration of the body. A distinctive set of measurement challenges concern the articulation of consent. In the context of few successful prosecutions of rape[190], there have been attempts to reform the legal framework[191]. This has implications for the categories in which statistics on rape and other forms of sexual violence are collected.

Definition

The international legal standard for the definition of rape is established by UN-authorised courts drawing on the *Universal Declaration of Human Rights*. In the 47 Member States of the Council of Europe,

---

[190] Lovett, J. and Kelly, L. (2009) *Different Systems, Similar Outcomes: Tracking Attrition in Reported Rape Cases across Europe.* London, Child and Woman Abuse Studies Unit, London Metropolitan University.

[191] McGlynn, C. (2008) 'Rape as "torture"? Catherine MacKinnon and questions of feminist strategy', *Feminist Legal Studies*, 16: 71–85; Yung, C. (2014) 'Rape law fundamentals', *Yale Journal of Law & Feminism*, 27: 1–46.

the European Court of Human Rights has developed jurisprudence to implement the *European Convention of Human Rights*, itself based on the *Universal Declaration of Human Rights*. In conflict zones, the jurisprudence of specially established International War Crimes Tribunals draws additionally on the Rome Statute of the International Criminal Court and other international conventions concerning conduct in war.

The definitions of rape used by national legal systems and by administrative and survey sources have been adapting to these international legal developments, but often with a time lag. As a consequence, there are variations in the definition of rape used in administrative and survey statistics in the EU[192], wider Europe[193] and beyond, with implications for the quality of comparative data[194]. The realignment of statistical categories to meet the standards laid down in international law and jurisprudence is required.

The definition of rape now centres on the lack of consent to penetration of the body that violates sexual autonomy. The concept of the non-consensual violation of sexual autonomy is at the heart of the definition of rape. The definition of rape also deems the penetration of some orifices of the body to be inherently sexual, thereby distinguishing it from bodily harm in assault and thus recognising the damage to the sexual autonomy of the victim.

The focus on consent entails the rejection of the notion that force is necessary to the definition of rape and includes issues concerning

[192]   EC (2010) *Feasibility Study to Assess the Possibilities, Opportunities and Needs to Standardise National Legislation on Violence against Women, Violence against Children and Sexual Orientation Violence*. Brussels, EC; Lovett, J. and Kelly, L. (2009) *Op cit.* Footnote 190.

[193]   Aebi, M., Akdeniz, G., Barclay, G., Campistol, C., Caneppele, S., Gruszczyńska, B., Harrendorf, S., Heiskanen, M., Hysi, V., Jehle, J., Jokinen, A., Kensey, A., Killias, M., Lewis, C., Savona, E., Smit, P. and Þórisdóttir, R. (2014) *European Sourcebook on Crime and Criminal Justice Statistics*. 5th ed. Helsinki, HEUNI.

[194]   Harrendorf, S. (2012) 'Offence definitions in the European Sourcebook of Crime and Criminal Justice Statistics and their influence on data quality and comparability', *European Journal on Criminal Policy and Research*, 18: 23–53; Walby, S., Olive, P., Towers, J., Francis, B., Strid, S., Krizsán, A., Lombardo, E., May-Chahal, C., Franzway, S., Sugarman, D., Agarwal, B. and Armstrong, J. (2015) *Stopping Rape: Towards a Comprehensive Policy*. Bristol, Policy Press.

inability to consent. The gendering of rape has also been changing: both de-gendering (through the inclusion of a wider range of pertinent body parts and rejection of the marital exemption) and re-gendering (by the introduction of legal distinctions between victims on the grounds of their sex).

Rape is the penetration of the body in the absence of consent that violates sexual autonomy. In international law, rape does not require the use of force, threat or coercion. Inability to consent through unconsciousness or intoxication or abuse of authority meets the criteria of absence of consent. Coercion in conflict zones obviates the need to prove lack of consent.

The definition of sexual assault shares with rape the component of touching without freely given consent that violates sexual autonomy. Unlike rape, it does not require penetration.

Consent not force

The European Court of Human Rights[195] ruled that sexual intercourse without genuine free consent violates protection of the sexual autonomy of the victim and is rape. The absence of force, struggle, blackmail, terror or threat from the perpetrator or lack of physical resistance by the victim is held not to constitute proof of non-consent to intercourse.

The *Istanbul Convention* defines rape as 'engaging in non-consensual vaginal, anal or oral penetration of a sexual nature of the body of another person with any bodily part or object'[196]. The foregrounding of consent in defining rape that is invoked in contemporary human rights case law can be traced through centuries of legal tradition. For example, in England, consent has been recognised as the defining difference between rape and consensual sexual intercourse since 1285[197]. Consent was central to one of the first published legal

---

[195] *M.C. v Bulgaria*, ECtHR 2004, no. 39272/98.
[196] Council of Europe (2011) *Op cit.* Footnote 47.
[197] Pollock, F. and Maitland, F. (1895) *The History of English Law before the Time of Edward I: In Two Volumes.* Indianapolis, Liberty Fund (2012).

definitions of rape: 'ravishing of a woman, dame or damsel whether ... neither assented before or after'[198]. This continues in current law: when a person 'agrees [to intercourse] by choice, and has the freedom and capacity to make that choice' (section 74)[199]. Circumstances that mean consent is not possible in law have included the use of violence or fear of violence, the victim being asleep, unconscious or having been administered a stupefying substance and where disability prevents the victim from being able to communicate consent[200].

Developments in legal rulings on consent not force have been supported politically, though unevenly. For example, the European Parliament 2009 Resolution states that lack of consent should be central in domestic rape legislation and jurisprudence: 'agreement by choice when having the freedom and capacity to make that choice'[201]. Nevertheless, some European countries have retained force and violence as constituents of their rape definitions[202] and are thus out of alignment with the *European Convention on Human Rights*, of which they are signatories.

While the earlier definition of rape still applies in conflict zones, it is also recognised that the generally coercive environment means it is not necessary to separately prove the lack of consent of the victim. For example, the International Criminal Tribunal on Yugoslavia (ICTY) Appeal Chamber recognised rapes as 'serious violations of sexual autonomy [which] are to be penalised'[203] and defined rape and consent with regard to the intention (*mens rea*) of the perpetrator in criminal rape:

[198] Hale, M. (1736) *Historia Placitorum Coronæ (The History of the Pleas of the Crown): In Two Volumes.* 1st ed. London, Savoy Nutt and Gosling: 627.

[199] HM Government (2003) *Sexual Offences Act 2003.* www.legislation.gov.uk/ukpga/2003/42/contents [November 2016].

[200] Lovett, J. and Kelly, L. (2009) *Op cit:* 43. Footnote 190.

[201] European Parliament (2009) *Resolution 1691 on the Rape of Women, including Marital Rape Following Assembly Debate on 2 October 2009.*

[202] Forowicz, M. (2010) *The Reception of International Law in the European Court of Human Rights.* Oxford, Oxford University Press.

[203] *Prosecutor v. Kunarac, Kovac and Vukovic,* ICTY 2002, nos. IT-96-23 and IT-96-23/1-A.

where such sexual penetration occurs without the consent of the victim. Consent for this purpose must be consent given voluntarily, as a result of the victim's free will, assessed in the context of the surrounding circumstances. The mens rea is the intention to effect this sexual penetration, and the knowledge that it occurs without the consent of the victim[204].

The International Criminal Tribunal for Rwanda (ICTR) in the Muhimana case in 2005[205] ruled that 'coercion is an element that may obviate the relevance of consent as an evidentiary factor in the crime of rape' in the context of war and conflict. The ICTR judgment in Akayesu[206] defined rape as 'a physical invasion of a sexual nature committed on a person under circumstances which are coercive', where coercive can be understood as 'inherent in ... armed conflict or military presence of threatening forces on an ethnic basis'[207].

Age

There are variations in the age at which the victim is considered legally able to consent to sex, younger than which the victim may be treated as raped. There are also variations in the age at which a person can be regarded as criminally responsible. Statutory rape is understood in law as intercourse with a child below the age at which they cannot legally consent. The *Lanzarote Convention*[208] protects children and young people from sexual abuse up to the age of 18. However, in practice, within Europe the age of consent varies from 13 to 17 and there are

---

[204] *Prosecutor v. Furundzija*, ICTY 1998, no. IT-95-17/1-T.
[205] *Prosecutor v Muhimana*, ICTR 2005, no. ICTR-95-1B-T.
[206] *Prosecutor v Jean-Paul Akayesu*, ICTR 1998, no. ICTR-96-4-T.
[207] MacKinnon, C (2006) *Op cit:* 237. Footnote 106.
[208] Council of Europe (2007) *Convention on the Protection of Children against Sexual Exploitation and Sexual Abuse Treaty Series: No. 201.* Lanzarote, signed 25 October. https://rm.coe.int/CoERMPublicCommonSearchServices/DisplayDCTMContent?documentId=0900001680084822 [November 2016].

gradations in the offence of rape that take the relative ages of victim and perpetrator into account[209].

Body parts

The traditional definition of rape was inherently gendered in the restriction of the relevant body parts to penis and vagina. The range of body parts that can be penetrated has been increased to include the vagina, mouth or anus and the addition of fingers and objects as well as a penis engaged in the penetration has removed the gendered nature of rape as involving a man's penis and a woman's vagina. This extension in the range of objects and orifices within the concept of rape de-genders the definition of rape in relation to both the victim and the perpetrator.

This extension of relevant body parts in the legal definition of rape has been adopted unevenly and slowly in different countries[210].

Relationship

Historically, the gender-saturated relationship of marriage was legally exempted from the law on rape, so a husband could violate the sexual autonomy of a wife with impunity. Over recent decades, the special treatment of marriage in the law on rape has been reduced around the world. Indeed, there has been the near-elimination of any exemption based on marital or partnership status in Europe. Criminalisation of marital rape across Europe was legislated in Sweden in 1965 (as a sexual violation); Ireland in 1990; England and Wales in 1991; France in 1992, Germany and Hungary in 1997 and Greece in 2006 (as a form

---

[209]   Aebi, M. et al. (2014) *Op cit.* Footnote 193; Lovett, J. and Kelly, L. (2009) *Op cit.* Footnote 190.

[210]   Stern, V. (2010) *The Stern Review.* London, Government Equalities Office. http://webarchive.nationalarchives.gov.uk/20100418065537/http://equalities.gov.uk/PDF/Stern_Review_acc_FINAL.pdf [November 2016]; Aebi, M. et al. (2014) *Op cit.* Footnote 193.

of domestic violence)[211]. Other areas followed a little later (after 2000), including Cambodia, Thailand, Rwanda and Ghana[212]. Nevertheless, marital rape remains legal in many countries[213].

Sex of victim

The crime category of rape is re-gendered by a new distinction between rape of women and rape of men, introduced at the level of legal codes. Data is thus necessarily collected on this basis, thereby providing counts of the number of recorded rapes of women and rapes of men.

This innovation constitutes a precedent in providing a mechanism that enables the easy and accurate disaggregation of violence against women and men. It is highly recommended and should be replicated for all other forms of violence.

Implications for measurement

Statistical categories used by the UN (UNODC ICCS) and European entities (European Sourcebook) are not in alignment with international and European law and jurisprudence. They should be. For example, the definition of rape used by the European Sourcebook for gathering statistics is 'sexual intercourse with a person against her/his will (per vaginam or other)'[214]. This does not match international legal definitions; the concept of 'consent' is absent and the list of 'body parts' is insufficient. The UNODC ICCS still distinguishes between rape with force and rape without force:

> Sexual penetration without valid consent or with consent as a result of intimidation, force, fraud, coercion, threat, deception,

---

[211] EC (2010) *Op cit.* Footnote 57; Lovett, J. and Kelly, L. (2009) *Op cit.* Footnote 190.
[212] Walby, S. et al. (2015) *Op cit.* Footnote 194.
[213] Walby, S. et al. (2015) *Op cit.* Footnote 194.
[214] Harrendorf, S. (2012) *Op cit:* 29. Footnote 194.

use of drugs or alcohol, abuse of power or of a position of vulnerability, or the giving or receiving of benefits ... . where Sexual penetration, at minimum, is the penetration of the vulva, anus or mouth with any body part or object[215].

This reference to force should be removed and a single category, as in international law, should be in use.

In cases of statutory rape, both the UNODC and European Sourcebook collect data based on the age of consent in each State, despite the recommendation of the *Lanzarote Convention*[216]. Further, the current exclusion of sexual assault of a child without force[217] should be addressed in European rape statistics.

Circumstances in which victims cannot give consent are currently covered by the European Sourcebook as 'sexual intercourse without force with a helpless person' and are collected in all countries[218]. The UNODC definition includes rape 'as a result of intimidation, force, fraud, coercion, threat, deception, use of drugs or alcohol, abuse of power or of a position of vulnerability, or the giving or receiving of benefits'[219]. In light of jurisprudence and developments in legislation, international statistical definitions should be updated to include rape where the victim was 'asleep, unconscious, or otherwise at risk of harm.' Another aggravating factor is perpetrators who stop a woman with an impairment or health condition from withdrawing her consent by taking away equipment she uses to be independent, or by using the victim's impairment or condition to sexually penetrate her when consent cannot be freely given.

In the ICCS[220], the definition of rape excludes 'Acts of abuse of a position of ... trust ... for profiting financially, physically, socially or politically from the – prostitution or sexual acts of a person' which

---

[215] UNODC (2015) *Op cit:* 50. Footnote 33.
[216] Council of Europe (2007) *Op cit.* Footnote 208.
[217] Aebi, M. et al. (2014) *Op cit:* 385. Footnote 193.
[218] Aebi, M. et al. (2014) *Op cit:* 384. Footnote 193.
[219] UNODC (2015) *Op cit:* 50. Footnote 33.
[220] UNODC (2015) *Op cit.* Footnote 33.

are only classified as sexual exploitation or 'injurious acts of a sexual nature,' rather than being classified as rape. The European Court of Human Rights (ECtHR)[221] is clear that consent is impossible in detention, war and genocide, so sexual penetration in the circumstances presented earlier should not be excluded from the rape definition. Rape in coercive circumstances could be included in the UNODC classification.

Rape in marriage is now recognised in international law and in all EU Member States, but the European Sourcebook includes these crimes as 'violent intra-marital sexual intercourse'. They should instead be categorised as rape.

Future data collection should use definitions of rape that are in alignment with international law. However, rape is still under-reported to administrative bodies and conviction rates remain low, so administrative data alone is not an appropriate source of data on the rate of rape.

FEMALE GENITAL MUTILATION

Introduction

Female Genital Mutilation (FGM) refers to procedures to partially or totally remove the external female genitalia, or other injury to the female organ, for non-medical reasons[222]. FGM[223] is a form of violent crime in need of specific measurement, even though it could be subsumed within 'assault', because of its serious and distinctive harms. The definition of FGM is intended to be workable for statistical purposes, while being rooted in international law. Particular challenges

---

[221] *Aydın v Turkey*, ECtHR 1997, no. 23178/94.

[222] WHO (1997) *Eliminating FGM: An Interagency Statement. OHCHR, UNAIDS, UNDP, UNECA, UNESCO, UNFPA, UNHCR, UNICEF, WHO.* Geneva, WHO. www.un.org/womenwatch/daw/csw/csw52/statements_missions/Interagency_Statement_on_Eliminating_FGM.pdf [November 2016].

[223] EIGE (2013) *Female Genital Mutilation in the European Union and Croatia.* Vilnius, EIGE.

concern the minimum threshold and a definition for use across criminal justice, health, education and social services[224].

The legal and policy framework of FGM is under development within the UN[225], Council of Europe[226] and the EU[227] and FGM is increasingly recognised as a criminal act. In some states, a specific criminal law has been introduced to address FGM (for example, the UK and Sweden) whereas other countries (for example, France) have included FGM in existing legislation, either as a subcategory within another form of violence or by applying existing legal provisions dealing with bodily injury; serious bodily injury; voluntary corporal lesions; mutilation; and/or the removal of organs or body tissue[228]. There is also legislation requiring the reporting of FGM to the police in the UK and Sweden.

The tension between naming and making a specific form of violence visible in order to combat it and the risk that this stigmatises the group in which it is prevalent should be recognised; this is parallel to that concerning forced marriage and other forms of intersectional violence against women[229].

[224] EIGE (2015a) *Estimation of Girls at Risk of Female Genital Mutilation.* Vilnius, EIGE.

[225] UN (2009) *Overview of Legislation in the European Union to Address Female Genital Mutilation: Challenges and Recommendations for the Implementation of Laws.* Expert paper prepared by Els Leye and Alexia Sabbe, UNDAW/UNECA. www.un.org/womenwatch/daw/egm/vaw_legislation_2009/Expert%20Paper%20EGMGPLHP%20_Els%20Leye_.pdf [November 2016].

[226] Council of Europe (2001) *Female Genital Mutilation.* Parliamentary Assembly Resolution 1247; Council of Europe (2011) *Op cit.* Footnote 47.

[227] European Parliament (2008) *European Parliament Resolution Towards an EU Strategy on Rights of the Child.* http://www.europarl.europa.eu/sides/getDoc.do?pubRef=-//EP//TEXT+TA+P6-TA-2008-0012+0+DOC+XML+V0//EN [November 2016]; European Parliament (2009) *European Parliament Resolution on Female Genital Mutilation.* www.europarl.europa.eu/sides/getDoc.do?type=TA&reference=P5-TA-2001-0476&format=XML&language=EN [November 2016]; EIGE (2013) *Op. Cit.* Footnote 223; EIGE (2015a) *Op. Cit.* Footnote 224; EIGE (2015b) *Estimation of Girls at Risk of Female Genital Mutilation in the EU: A Step-by-Step Guide.* Vilnius, EIGE.

[228] UN (2009) *Op cit.* Footnote 225; EIGE (2013) *Op cit.* Footnote 223.

[229] Crenshaw, K. (1991) *Op cit.* Footnote 126; Strid, S., Walby, S. and Armstrong, J. (2013) 'Intersectionality and multiple inequalities: visibility in British policy on violence against women', *Social Politics,* 20: 558–81.

Definition

FGM practices are variously referred to as mutilation, circumcision, cutting, genital surgery and related terms. Johnsdotter and Essen[230] argue the terms 'cutting' or 'circumcision' are less stigmatising than 'mutilation', as is the term 'surgery'[231]. 'Mutilation' is more widely used by researchers in the social sciences, law and criminology, by activists and in policy documents in western countries and by the WHO, since it emphasises the violating nature of and injury caused by these practices[232], which are a violation of women's human rights in the *European Convention of Human Rights* (ECHR); the *EU Charter on Human Rights*; the *Convention on the Elimination of Discrimination against Women* (CEDAW); the *International Covenant on Civil and Political Rights* (ICCPR); the *International Convention on Economic, Social and Cultural Rights* (ICESCR), the *Convention on the Rights of the Child* (CRC) and the *Convention Against Torture* (CAT).

For measurement purposes, several definitional issues emerge. Should FGM be defined in the widest possible sense so as to capture the full range of practices, or more narrowly so as to target specifically injurious types? Should the definition focus on force and perpetrator, or injury and victim? And what are the implications of either a wide or a narrow definition of FGM for reporting and recording data, for developing indicators and for the law?

The *Istanbul Convention* (Article 38) defines FGM as:

---

[230]   Johnsdotter, S. and Essen, B. (2015) 'Cultural change after migration: circumcision of girls in Western migrant communities', *Best Practice & Research Clinical Obstetrics & Gynaecology*, 32: 15-25.

[231]   Public Policy Advisory Network on Female Genital Mutilation Surgeries in Africa (2012) 'Seven things to know about female genital surgeries in Africa', *Hastings Centre Report*, 6: 19–27; Obermeyer, C. (1999) 'Female genital surgeries: the known, the unknown and the unknow-able', *Medical Anthropology Quarterly*, 13: 79–106; Johnsdotter, S. (2012) 'Projected cultural histories of the cutting of female genitalia', *History and Anthropology*, 23: 91–114; Johnsdotter, S. and Essén, B. (2015) *Op cit.* Footnote 230.

[232]   EIGE (2013) *Op cit.* Footnote 223.

a excising, infibulating or performing any other mutilation to the whole or any part of a woman's labia majora, labia minora or clitoris; *b* coercing or procuring a woman to undergo any of the acts listed in point *a*; *c* inciting, coercing or procuring a girl to undergo any of the acts listed in point *a*[233].

The focus is on coercion.

The World Health Organisation[234] focuses on harm and identifies four types:

1. the partial or total removal of the clitoris and/or the prepuce (clitoridectomy);
2. he partial or total removal of the clitoris and the labia minora, with or without excision of the labia majora (excision);
3. the narrowing of the vaginal orifice with creation of a covering seal by cutting and appositioning the labia minora and/or the labia majora, with or without excision of the clitoris (infibulation);
4. 'unclassified': all other harmful procedures to the female genitalia for nonmedical purposes, for example, pricking, incising, scraping and cauterisation.

Types 1, 2 and 3 pose significant health problems while Type 4 may cause health problems, but not necessarily. All four types may be relevant to offences arising under national legislation (for example, the UK FGM Act 2003, the 1982 Swedish Act).

Three parallel trends are also relevant: first, the policy shift towards banning (in African countries) and criminalisation (in the EU); second, the decrease in the overall levels of FGM[235] and a shift towards

---

233 Council of Europe (2011) *Op cit.* Footnote 47.

234 WHO (1997) *Op cit.* Footnote 222; WHO (2011) *An Update on WHO's Work on female Genital Mutilation.* Progress report. Geneva, WHO; WHO (2014) *Op cit.* Footnote 14.

235 Johnsdotter, S. and Essen, B. (2015) *Op cit.* Footnote 230; Yoder, P. and Khan, S. (2008) *Numbers of Women Circumcised in Africa.* DHS working paper 38. Geneva, World Health Organisation. http://www.who.int/reproductivehealth/publications/fgm/dhs_report/en/.

'milder forms' of FGM[236]; and third, the increase in the number of mutilated women within the EU due to increased migration from FGM-practicing countries[237]. There is a trend towards the practice of 'milder' forms (Type 4) of FGM following migration[238].

The increasing practice of female genital cosmetic surgery in western cultures also needs to be considered[239], as this practice can be regarded as Type 4 FGM. Considering milder forms of practices as FGM while excluding 'western' practices such as piercing, tattooing and labiaplasty/plastic genital surgery raises issues of double standards and cultural relativism. Arguments used in favour of distinguishing between the two include that, in the former case, the practice (regardless of type) is almost exclusively performed on underage girls (with or without consent is irrelevant as the girls are underage and therefore cannot consent in the meaning of the law), the consequences are physically harmful and sometimes life-threatening and the purpose or intent is to control girls' and women's sexuality and maintain girls' purity in preparation for marriage[240]. In cases of piercing or labiaplasty, the purpose is rather the opposite: to enhance women's self-esteem and sexual experiences (see Lowenstein et al.[241] for physicians' attitudes on

---

[236] Hodes, D., Armitage, A. and Dykes, A. (2014) 'G165 female genital mutilation in London and the UNICEF report: a local perspective on worldwide statistics', *Archives of Disease in Childhood*, 99(1): A73–A73.

[237] Avalos, L. (2014) *Female Genital Mutilation and Designer Vaginas in Britain: Crafting an Effective Legal and Policy Framework*. University of Arkansas research paper: 14–25; European Parliament (2009) *Op cit*. Footnote 201.

[238] UNICEF (2013) *Female Genital Mutilation: A Statistical Overview and Exploration of the Dynamics of Change*. UNICEF Publications, 184; EIGE (2015a) *Op cit*. Footnote 224.

[239] Avalos, L. (2014) *Op cit*. Footnote 237; Barbara, G., et al., (2015) '"The first cut is the deepest": a psychological, sexological and gynaecological perspective on female genital cosmetic surgery', *Acta Obstetricia et Gynecologica Scandinavica*, 94(9): 915–920; Kelly, B. and Foster, C. (2012) 'Should female genital cosmetic surgery and genital piercing be regarded ethically and legally as female genital mutilation?' *BJOG: An International Journal of Obstetrics and Gynaecology*, 119: 389–92.

[240] EIGE (2015a) *Op cit*. Footnote 224.

[241] Lowenstein, L., Salonia, A., Schechter, A., Porst, H., Burri, A. and Reisman, Y. (2014) 'Physicians' attitude towards female genital surgery: a multinational survey', The *Journal of Sex Medicine*, 11: 33–9.

this issue). The practice is generally performed on consenting adults, although there are exceptions[242].

A wide definition of FGM includes any procedures and surgery performed on genitalia for non-medical reasons. Such a definition would include female genital cosmetic surgery, tattoos and piercings. Where these practices involve children this may also be a breach of the CRC[243]. However, a wide definition misses the distinctions and nuances between forced and voluntary, between alteration and injury. A disadvantage of a broad definition is the issue of reporting: health practitioners report difficulty in recognising FGM and in distinguishing it from natural variations[244].

FGM can be more narrowly defined as procedures involving the partial or total removal of the external female genitalia or any other injury to the female genital organs for non-medical reasons[245]. Here, the focus is on injury and the victim. The definition of FGM could focus even more narrowly on the use of force; that is, 'forced FGM', as in the Council of Europe[246] Article 38, in which the Council urges states to criminalise the coercion of a woman to undergo the excising, infibulating or performing of any other mutilation to the whole or any part of a woman's labia majora, labia minora or clitoris (see Nussbaum[247] for the use of physical force on children as the key moral issue with FGM). The advantage of a narrow definition is the improvement in ability to recognise that FGM has taken place and thus also in the consistency and accuracy of measurement.

Units of measurement

The units of measurement should include event, victim and perpetrator. The current focus is on the number of victims. Some attention is paid

---

[242] Saracoglu, M., Zengin, T., Ozturk, H. and Genc, M. (2014) 'Female genital mutilation/cutting type 4', *Journal of Andrology and Gynaecology*, 2: 5–10.

[243] European Parliament (2008) *Op cit*. Footnote 227.

[244] Hodes, D. et al. (2014) *Op cit*. Footnote 236.

[245] WHO (1997) *Op cit*. Footnote 222.

[246] Council of Europe (2011) *Op cit*. Footnote 47.

[247] Nussbaum, M. (1999) *Sex and Social Justice*. Oxford, Oxford University Press.

to the perpetrators, but the identification of perpetrators is complex. While the focus of the authorities is usually on the parents, since they are the ones who decide a girl is to be cut (though it might be difficult to identify the decision-making powers of each parent), the 'cutter' will (usually) not be the parent[248].

FGM is also not necessarily a one-off event. When women are re-infibulated after giving birth, FGM is a repeat event.

Data collection and coordination

The issues in data collection at national levels concern: a general lack of existing data on non-permanent residents, in some cases due to what are perceived as ethical issues in registering data; sample size, the numbers being too small to be statistically relevant in survey data; obligatory/non-obligatory reporting by health practitioners; self-reporting; and repeat injury/mutilation (re-infibulation).

FGM is not necessarily named as such in the penal code, but can be 'hidden' under crime codes such as 'aggravated assault', 'grave bodily injury' or other applicable categories or codes.

There is little robust data at national level on the prevalence of FGM[249], though there are methods for producing estimates of the number of girls at risk[250]. The most common method is to apply the national FGM prevalence rate for specific age groups in the country of origin (respectively origin of parents) and apply these to the number of women/daughters of migrant residents in the country, region or city of immigration[251]. However, this ignores the (significant) effects of migration on the practice[252].

[248] EIGE (2015a) Op cit. Footnote 224.
[249] EIGE (2013) Op cit. Footnote 223.
[250] EIGE (2015a) Op cit. Footnote 224; EIGE (2015b) Op cit. Footnote 227.
[251] EIGE (2013) Op cit. Footnote 223.
[252] Johnsdotter, S. and Essen, B. (2015) Op cit. Footnote 230; EIGE (2015a) Op cit. Footnote 224.

Implications for measurement

There are three main challenges for measuring FGM[253].

First, data collection is fragmented across different bodies: child protection; health/medical/hospital; police, justice and immigration authorities. The estimation of the scale of FGM requires fine-grained knowledge of nationality, country or region of origin or ethnicity, since these different collectivities have different rates of FGM. This information is also hard to gain with accuracy. The estimation of FGM also requires information about the age at which FGM is performed in the country of origin, which may not accurately reflect the age at which FGM is performed in host countries. Data from administrative bodies is unreliable and data collection through surveys poses difficulties in a European context, since the sample would need to be representative of the many different migrant communities (taking ethnicity into account) living in the country/region. Randomised surveys would be unlikely to capture the relevant minority communities. Furthermore, self-reporting by women has proven inaccurate; women often do not know which type – following the WHO definition – of FGM they have[254].

Second, active detection of FGM by health professionals by means of gynaecological examinations or check-ups poses ethical issues. There are difficulties in recognising and categorising FGM by health practitioners[255], in addition to evidence that FGM actually may be carried out by health professionals[256].

Third, data on FGM is currently rarely collected, even when detected in health or education settings. There are advantages to making the collection of this data more consistent through mandatory reporting; for example, the new UK FGM Data Enhanced Collection

---

[253] EIGE (2015a) *Op cit.* Footnote 224; EIGE (2015b) *Op cit.* Footnote 227.
[254] Simpson, J., Robinson, K., Creighton, S. and Hodes, D. (2012) 'Female genital mutilation: the role of health professionals in prevention, assessment and management', *British Medical Journal*, 344: e1361.
[255] Obermeyer, C. (2005) *Op cit.* Footnote 231.
[256] Paliwal, P. (2014) 'Management of type III female genital mutilation in Birmingham, UK: A retrospective audit', *Midwifery*, 30: 282–8.

means that NHS healthcare professionals will be legally obliged to submit information on every woman with FGM attending the NHS[257]. However, even though data will not be released to third parties such as the police, the mandatory submission of highly sensitive information without patient consent risks damaging trust in health professionals[258].

FGM needs to be named as such in policy and criminal law. Since any type of FGM constitutes injury and a violation of human rights, it might appear logical to adopt a broad definition. However, even though milder forms of FGM (for example, pricking or incising) remain injurious and a breach of human rights, 'counting' their occurrences does not seem realistic since the injury is often not visible post factum and the victim does not necessarily know it has happened to them. The large-scale estimates of FGM prevalence in countries of origin do not include Type 4 practices; thus, Type 4 (following the WHO definition) should be excluded from the definition and from data collection. This means also excluding genital cosmetic surgery.

Further forms to be taken into account

Introduction to further forms

There are several further forms of violence and coercion, named in the Istanbul and other relevant Conventions, which need to be taken into account: stalking, forced marriage, sexual harassment, trafficking in human beings, forced prostitution, and forced sterilisation. A brief definition of each is given below.

---

[257] Home Office (2015) *Mandatory Reporting of Female Genital Mutilation: Procedural Information*. London, Home Office.

[258] Bewley, S. (2015) 'Mandatory submission of patient identifiable information to third parties: FGM now, what next?' *British Medical Journal*, H5146; Dyer, C. (2014) 'Acute hospitals in England will have to report cases of female genital mutilation from September', *British Medical Journal*, 348: 1433.

Stalking

Stalking is defined in Article 34 of the *Istanbul Convention*[259] as 'repeatedly engaging in threatening conduct directed at another person, causing her or him to fear for her or his safety'. It is a course of conduct made up of a series of events. Stalking crosses the threshold of violence as a consequence of the threat that causes fear for safety. It is a crime in many countries. Measurement needs the use of all three units of event, victim and perpetrator. Data is currently collected from both the criminal justice system (since it is a crime) and some population surveys; for example, the Crime Survey for England and Wales (CSEW).

Forced marriage

A forced marriage is one in which one or both people do not, or cannot, consent to the marriage. This is not the same as an arranged marriage to which both parties consented. The force can be physical violence or non-physical coercion. In 2013, the UN Human Rights Council passed a Resolution against child, early and forced marriages, naming these as a violation of human rights. The *Istanbul Convention* also names forced marriage as a form of violence. Many countries have legislated against forced marriage; for example, the UK made forced marriage a criminal offence in The Anti-Social Behaviour, Crime and Policing Act 2014[260].

There are attempts to measure forced marriage[261]. The unit of measurement is most often victims: those forced to marry. Most statistics are disaggregated by the sex of the victim and also by the age of the victim in order to separate child marriage from forced marriage

---

[259]   Council of Europe (2011) *Op cit.* Footnote 47.

[260]   UK Government (2014) *Anti-Social Behaviour, Crime and Policing Act 2014.* www.legislation.gov.uk/ukpga/2014/12/contents/enacted [November 2016].

[261]   Walby, S., Armstrong, J. and Strid, S. (2012) 'Developing measures of multiple forms of sexual violence and their contested treatment in the criminal justice system', in Brown, J. and Walklate, S. (eds) *Handbook on Sexual Violence*. London, Routledge: 90-113.

of adults. For example, the UN Children's Fund (UNICEF) publishes statistics on child marriage[262]. Individual countries publish statistics drawn from administrative sources, including the UK Forced Marriage Unit[263]. There are small-scale studies and also attempts to use survey methods to measure forced marriage in countries where this is more common, including South Asia[264]. While the focus on victims should be maintained, the unit of measurement should additionally include events (marriages) and perpetrators. There are likely to be multiple perpetrators operating in complex systems of family and kin. Whether the other partner in the marriage is also a perpetrator depends on whether they know their spouse was forced.

While most current statistics derive from administrative authorities, additional sources could include data from services for victims and victim surveys.

Sexual harassment

Sexual harassment is defined in the *Istanbul Convention* as 'any form of unwanted verbal, non-verbal or physical conduct of a sexual nature with the purpose or effect of violating the dignity of a person, in particular when creating an intimidating, hostile, degrading, humiliating or offensive environment'. It is illegal in most countries, though usually under employment law rather than criminal law. It may be conceptualised more usually as coercion than as violence. The US Equal Employment Opportunity Commission (EEOC) states: '[I]t is unlawful to harass a person (an applicant or employee) because of that person's sex.' Sexual harassment is illegal in the EU since it is included

---

[262]   UNICEF. *Child Marriage.* http://data.unicef.org/child-protection/child-marriage.html [November 2016].

[263]   Home Office (2016) *Forced Marriage Unit Statistics 2015.* London, Home Office. www.gov.uk/government/uploads/system/uploads/attachment_data/file/505827/Forced_Marriage_Unit_statistics_2015.pdf [November 2016].

[264]   For example, a national survey of forced marriage in South Asia: SALCO (South Asian Legal Clinic of Ontario) (2012) Forced Marriage National. www.springtideresources.org/resource/forced-marriage-national-survey-south-asian-legal-clinic-ontario [November 2016].

within the definition of discrimination in Directive 2002/73/EC Equal Treatment in Access to Employment[265]. In the EU, a distinction is made between sexual harassment and gender harassment; both are illegal under employment law.

Because it is illegal, some statistics on sexual harassment that are reported to authorities are available from administrative sources. In addition, trade unions and other employee organisations[266], civil society organisations[267] and other bodies[268] conduct surveys of sexual harassment in specific contexts, though reliable national- level data is under-developed. Sexual harassment is typically measured by number of victims; however, the unit of measurement should be expanded to also include events and perpetrators.

Trafficking in human beings

Trafficking in human beings entails the control and exploitation of one person by another and is a crime under international law[269], the Council of Europe, the EU and most countries. Trafficking does not include force as a necessary part of its definition. The coercion may take non-violent forms; hence, it can straddle the boundary of violence/not-violence.

Trafficking is most often measured through a focus on victims. Sometimes these statistics are disaggregated by the sex and age of the victim in order to identify children. For example, Eurostat[270] publishes data on the number of victims of trafficking identified in EU Member

[265]   European Commission (2007) *Directive 2002/73/EC: Equal Treatment in Access to Employment*. www.equalrightstrust.org/content/eu-directive-200273ec-equal-treatment-access-employment [November 2016].

[266]   See, for example, Trades Union Congress (TUC) (2016) *Still Just a Bit of Banter?* London, Trade Union Congress. www.tuc.org.uk/sites/default/files/SexualHarassmentreport2016.pdf [November 2016].

[267]   See, for example, the End Violence Against Women (EVAW) coalition's survey of sexual harassment: www.endviolenceagainstwomen.org.uk/sexual-harassment [November 2016].

[268]   EU Agency for Fundamental Rights (2014) *Op cit.* Footnote 68.

[269]   UN (2000) *Op cit.* Footnote 32.

[270]   Eurostat (2015) *Trafficking in Human Beings.* Statistical Working Paper. Brussels, Eurostat.

States disaggregated by the sex of the victim, the form of trafficking and the age of the victim.

Trafficking usually involves several perpetrators since it is a form of serious and organised crime, often drawing on complex systems of kin, communities and criminals. Statistics on perpetrators are available from criminal justice authorities and published in various formats by national statistical offices, UNODC and Eurostat[271].

There are ongoing developments to address the serious challenges involved in measurement[272]. These include devising survey methodologies in source countries to estimate the number of victims and innovative statistical techniques to improve estimates from fragmentary data[273].

Forced prostitution

Forced prostitution entails the control of one person over another to force or coerce that person into non-consensual sexual activity; it is illegal in most countries. Forced prostitution is named in the *Inter-American Convention on the Prevention, Punishment and Eradication of Violence against Women 'Convention of Belem do Para'*[274]. Forced prostitution overlaps with trafficking for sexual exploitation since it is the exploitation of the prostitution of others. Both forced prostitution and trafficking for sexual exploitation are criminally illegal in international and most national law.

Measurement challenges are similar to those for trafficking in human beings. There are useful though limited statistics from criminal justice sources and small-scale studies. Defining the boundary distinction between forced and non-forced prostitution is a major challenge.

---

[271]   Eurostat (2015) *Op cit.* Footnote 270.
[272]   Walby, S., Apitzsch, B., Armstrong, J., Balderston, S., Follis, K., Francis, B., Kelly, L., May-Chahal, C., Rashid, A., Shire, K., Towers, J. and Tunte, M. (2016) *The Gender Dimension of Trafficking in Human Beings*. Brussels, European Commission.
[273]   For example the capture-recapture method.
[274]   Organisation of American States (1994) *Op cit.* Footnote 48.

Forced sterilisation

Sterilisation that is practiced without full, free and informed consent is forced (also termed coercive or involuntary). Forced sterilisation severely limits or removes the fertility and reproductive rights of women and girls. It occurs when the procedure is carried out despite a woman expressly refusing, without her knowledge or when there is no opportunity to provide or withhold consent. Coerced sterilisation occurs when financial or other incentives, misinformation or intimidation are used to compel a woman to undergo the procedure.

The practice of sterilisation without consent constitutes a fundamental rights and a human rights violation[275]. Forced sterilisation breaches the right to health; bodily integrity; autonomy; privacy; security; found a family; and decide on the number and spacing of children[276]. Protections against forced sterilisation as torture and cruel, inhuman or degrading treatment also extend into the individual or private sphere[277].

International conventions[278] name forced sterilisation as a form of violence against women[279] because it disproportionately affects the rights, protections, freedoms and health of women and girls as a group. Forced sterilisation is also recognised as a form of medical and social

---

[275] UN (1995) *Op cit.* Footnote 31.

[276] UN (1999) *Report of the Special Rapporteur on Violence Against Women, its Causes and Consequences: Policies and Practices that Impact Women's Reproductive Rights and Contribute to, Cause or Constitute Violence against Women*, Report of Radika Coomaraswamy, 55th Session (UN Doc. E/CN.4/1999/68/Add.4, para. 51). New York, UN.

[277] UN General Assembly (2008) *Interim Report of the Special Rapporteur on Torture and Other Cruel, Inhuman or Degrading Treatment or Punishment*, Manfred Nowak (UN Doc A/63/175). New York, UN.

[278] Council of Europe (2011) *Op cit.* Footnote 47.

[279] UN (1992) *Op cit.* Footnote 29.

control[280] when it is perpetrated as part of systematic discrimination against groups with protected characteristics[281].

Domestic violence

Introduction

Domestic violence is named in the title of the *Istanbul Convention*, but is not identified as a specific form of violence in the same way as other forms. It is distinctive because of the relationship between perpetrator and victim. It potentially encompasses all of the forms of violence discussed in this chapter.

Definition

Domestic violence is challenging to define and measure because it straddles several of the conceptual distinctions conventionally made when measuring violence. It centres on violence from intimate partners and other family members, but may extend beyond this. Domestic means a current or former intimate partner (spouse, cohabitee, boyfriend/girlfriend) or family member. Violence includes all those forms defined and discussed in this chapter and defined in international and criminal law. In most countries, there is no single category in criminal law that exclusively captures all of the phenomena that together make up domestic violence. Domestic violence includes repetitions that challenge the traditional assumptions of one victim, one perpetrator and one event, as well as alignment between the action

---

[280]   UN Human Rights Council (2008) *Promotion and Protection of All Human Rights, Civil, Political, Economic, Social and Cultural Rights, Including the Right to Development: Report of the Special Rapporteur on Torture and Other Cruel, Inhuman or Degrading Treatment or Punishment*, Manfred Nowak. A/HRC/7/3 (paras. 38, 39). New York, UN.

[281]   UN Committee Against Torture (2009) *Concluding Observations: Slovakia* (UN Doc. CAT/C/SVK/CO/2, para 14); Czech Republic (UN Doc. CAT/C/CR/32/2, para 6(n)); Commissioner for Human Rights (2010) *Human Rights of Roma and Travellers in Europe*. Strasbourg: Council of Europe.

and the harm in both seriousness and temporality. There are challenges as to where the boundary between violence and not-violence is to be drawn. There are acts that only reach a criminal threshold when repeated. There are acts of coercion that may not cross the threshold of violence but do cross a criminal one, as in the case of 'coercive control', which has been demarcated as a 'crime' in some countries.

One approach to addressing the complicated nature of this assemblage is to attempt to create a new category in law to reflect the phenomenon; for example, coercive control. A different approach is to identify a core that is recognisable in traditional categories with limited revisions; for example, violence disaggregated by the relationship between perpetrator and victim and by the sex of the perpetrator and victim. There is active discussion as to whether domestic violence, or more particularly intimate partner violence, can be defined distinctively as a course of coercive conduct[282] or is better understood as a series of repeated acts, many of which are separate crimes[283]. In administrative statistics, a report for the European Commission finds that both approaches – a special category of crime and a particular aspect of existing crimes – exist in Member States[284].

The measurement of intimate partner violence in surveys is also varied; a specialised typology, the Conflict Tactics Scale[285], has been widely used in standalone surveys, while disaggregated crime categories are more frequently used when the relevant questions are asked as part of general crime surveys[286]. The variation between surveys in methodology and units of measurement as well as in the typology of forms has rendered comparisons between countries exceptionally

[282]   Myhill, A. (2015) 'Measuring coercive control', *Violence against Women*, 21: 355–75.

[283]   Walby, S., Towers, J. and Francis, B. (2014) *Op cit.* Footnote 90; Farrell, G., Phillips, C. and Pease, K. (1995) 'Like taking candy: why does repeat victimization occur?' *British Journal of Criminology*, 35: 384–99.

[284]   European Commission (2010) *Op cit.* Footnote 57.

[285]   Straus, M. (1999) 'The National Family Violence Surveys', in Straus, M. and Gelles, R. (eds) *Physical Violence in American Families.* 2nd ed. New Brunswick, Transaction Publishers: 3–16.

[286]   Walby, S., Towers, J. and Francis, B. (2014) *Op cit.* Footnote 90.

challenging. There have been attempts to address these challenges internationally[287] as well as in the EU[288].

There are variations in the definition of domestic violence that follow some of the same contours discussed earlier. The *Istanbul Convention* refers to violence against women and domestic violence (which includes violence against men). The violence might be restricted to that which is gender-motivated, or not. The treatment of domestic and intimate partner violence in both law and statistics may be a special unique category, or it may be constituted by the disaggregation of violent crime by the relationship between perpetrator and victim and by the sex of the victim.

Domestic violence: seriousness and repetition

Conflict Tactics Scale or crime codes

The Conflict Tactics Scale (CTS) is designed to measure differences between actions. Crime codes are designed to measure differences between events that are defined jointly as actions, harms and intentions.

The CTS was created to make distinctions concerning the tactics used to settle disputes in the domestic context. This list of 'tactics' ranged from rational argument to verbal aggression to the use of physical force[289]. Since its inception, the CTS has been subject to

---

[287] Breiding, M., Basile, K., Smith, S., Black, M. and Mahendra, R. (2015) *Intimate Partner Violence Surveillance and Uniform Definitions and recommended Data Elements*. Version 2.0. Atlanta, Centres for Disease Control and Prevention and National Centre for Injury Prevention and Control. www.cdc.gov/violenceprevention/pdf/intimatepartnerviolence.pdf [November 2016].

[288] Martinez, M. and Schröttle, M. with Condon, S., Springer-Kremser, M., Timmerman, G., Hagemann-White, C., Lenz, H., May-Chahal, C., Penhale, B., Reingardiene, P., Honkatukia, P., Jaspard, M., Lundgren, E., Piispa, M., Romito, P., Walby, S. and Westerstrand, J. (2006) *State of European Research on the Prevalence of Interpersonal Violence and its Impact on Health and Human Rights*. Report by the Coordinated Action on Human Rights Violations (CAHRV) to the European Commission, 6th Framework Programme, Project No. 506348.

[289] Straus, M. (1999) 'Measuring intrafamily conflict and violence: the Conflict Tactics Scales', in Straus, M. and Gelles, R. (eds) *Physical Violence in American Families*. 2nd ed. New Brunswick, Transaction Publishers: 29–45.

several revisions, with the addition of further actions and distinctions between them; however, its central feature – that it is a graded series of actions – remains constant. In some utilisations, additional sets of questions are included about injuries, but the form of these usually makes it very hard if not impossible to link injury to a specific action.

The CTS has been utilised in modified form in many victimisation surveys in addition to the Family Violence surveys of Straus and Gelles[290], including Demographic and Health Surveys (DHS)[291] carried out in over 25 countries with support from USAid[292], the International Violence against Women Surveys[293], the self-completion module on Intimate Violence in the CSEW[294] and the Fundamental Rights Agency EU Survey on Violence against Women[295]. The CTS does not address context[296]. Many have argued that ignoring context generates spurious gender symmetry in findings generated using this scale[297]. This context is one in which the violence from men to women is more likely to be frightening, controlling and injurious than that of violence from women to men.

[290] Straus, M. and Gelles, R. (1999) *Physical Violence in American Families*. 2nd ed. New Brunswick, Transaction Publishers.

[291] DHS. Domestic Violence module questionnaire for women. http://dhsprogram.com/pubs/pdf/DHSQM/DHS7_Module_DomViol_EN_15Jun2015_DHSQM.pdf [November 2016].

[292] DHS. *Gender Corner*. http://dhsprogram.com/topics/gender-Corner/index.cfm [November 2016].

[293] Johnson, H., Ollus, N. and Nevala, S. (2008) *Violence against Women: An International Perspective*. New York, Springer.

[294] ONS (2015) *Focus on Violent Crime and Sexual Offences: Intimate Personal Violence and Serious Sexual Assault*. Cardiff, ONS.

[295] FRA (2014) *Op cit*. Footnote 68.

[296] Dobash, R. and Dobash, R. (1992) *Op cit*. Footnote 16.

[297] Dobash, R., Dobash, R., Wilson, M. and Daly, M. (1992) 'The myth of sexual symmetry in marital violence', *Social Problems*, 39: 71–91; Johnson, M. (2008) *A Typology of Domestic Violence: Intimate Terrorism, Violent Resistance and Situational Couple Violence*. Lebanon, Northeastern University Press; Johnson, M. (1995) 'Patriarchal terrorism and common couple violence: two forms of violence against women', *Journal of Marriage and Family*, 57: 283–94; Towers, J., Walby, S. and Francis, B. (2014) *Op cit*. Footnote 90; Walby, S., Towers, J. and Francis, B. (2016) *Op cit*. Footnote 6; Planty, M. and Strom, K. (2007), 'Understanding the role of repeat victims in the production of annual US victimization rates', *Journal of Quantitative Criminology*, 23: 179–200.

There is a further, related problem with the CTS (including its modified forms): its incompatibility with criminal justice categories of crimes. The core categories of the CTS concern actions, not consequences. The concept of crime used in criminal justice systems includes consequences as well as actions. If an assault results in death, it is treated differently from if it leads to physical injury from which the victim can recuperate. Actions do not always align with consequences. In particular, there is a gendered mediation of the relationship between actions and injuries in which a specific action from a man to a woman is more likely to be physically injurious than the same action from a woman to a man. The British Crime Survey found that a minor act led to physical injury in 49% of the cases where the victim was female and 36% where the victim was male, and mental injury among 21% of female victims and 4% of male victims. It found that a severe act led to physical injury in 77% of cases where the victim was female and 56% when the victim was male, and mental injury in 42% of the cases where the victim was female and 11% where the victim was male[298]. This gendered lack of alignment between actions and harms is highly problematic. It means that actions alone should not be used to define a violent event (as is the case for the CTS).

In contrast, crimes are coded using information about not only actions, but also harms and intentions. The harms are often central to the definition, since these are the easiest to evidence objectively. Crime codes thus take account of the context (intention) and consequences (harms) of actions, thereby addressing a central criticism of the CTS. Crime codes are used throughout the criminal justice system and are widely understood in other policy systems. Crime victimisation surveys typically use crime codes as categories for defining violence; for example, the CSEW Victim Form module is based on crime codes so that the data collected by this part of the survey is comparable with data from the criminal justice system. In contrast, the data collected using the CTS is incompatible with that collected by the criminal justice system.

---

[298]   Walby, S. and Allen, J. (2004) *Op cit.* Footnote 81.

Thus, the CTS is not a suitable measurement scale. Instead, crime categories provide a better measure of domestic violence, including its seriousness, since they embed the injuries that are consequent on the actions. They also allow the disproportionate gender consequences of actions to be taken into account when measuring violence and for the alignment of findings from survey data with findings from administrative data. In addition, crime categories cover many forms of coercion that are not necessarily physical violence but that need to be included in the measurement framework, such as stalking.

Coercive control: 'repetition' and 'temporality'

Domestic violence is characterised by its repetitive nature; this needs to be addressed by the measurement framework. Collecting data about the repetition of violence against the same victim has been accorded little priority in traditional data collection instruments. The traditional assumption has often been one event, one victim, one perpetrator. Addressing repetition requires attention to the issue of 'temporality': the duration of the action, the duration of the consequences and the nature of the link between them. The temporality is both episodic (actions are events) and continuous (the harms persist over time). How is this to be addressed in the measurement framework? A further issue arises where each of the actions being repeated is small, not-violent and does not cross the criminal threshold, but the cumulative harm is substantial and this harm was intended.

In revising the traditional approach, two options have emerged. One option is to treat all the events as if they constitute a single course of conduct[299]. The other is to count each of the events and to treat each one as a violent crime when it crosses the criminal threshold[300]. Each pays attention to repetition and the duration of the harm. They differ in how they treat the multiplicity of the actions.

[299]   Kelly, L. (1988) *Surviving Sexual Violence*. Cambridge, Polity Press; Schechter, S. *Op cit*. Footnote 92; Stark, E. (2009) *Op cit*. Footnote 92.
[300]   Walby, S., Towers, J. and Francis, B. (2014) *Op cit*. Footnote 90; Walby, S., Towers, J. and Francis, B. (2016) *Op cit*. Footnote 6.

For Stark[301], 'coercive control' rather than violence is the key concept and focus. Coercive control is the harmful and unwarranted control of one human being by another, which is caused by a myriad of small actions. Coercive control can be established by the repetition of either physical or non-physical actions. Stark deploys the concept to distinguish between severe and non-severe forms of abuse of women, locating the severity of the abuse in the consequence (control) of the action rather than in the action itself. His focus is on the long duration of the consequences rather than the episodic nature of the repeated actions. Thus, coercive control is the danger, which might occur without physical violence.

Stark drew on the earlier work of Schechter on coercive control[302] and Kelly on the continuum of sexual violence[303]. Kelly's concept of continuum captures both the common character of the events loosely characterised as sexual violence and the interconnected nature of its different forms, which defy easy separate categorisation. The focus here is on the implications of many small actions (as well as large ones) for the enduring experiences of women and the overall environment within which women live. Laws on harassment and stalking criminalise repeated unwanted acts of communication that are intended to and do cause harm[304]. This encodes the concept of 'course of conduct' in law. The criminalisation of harassment and stalking was first applied outside of a cohabiting relationship. This is now expanding to cover intimate partnerships; for example, in Britain, recent legislation on coercive control effectively removes the exemption of cohabiting relationships from such criminalisation[305].

The implication of the concept of 'course of conduct' for measurement is to focus on counting victims and to treat each 'course of conduct' as if it were a single event, even though it occurs over a

---

[301] Stark, E. (2009) *Op cit*. Footnote 92.

[302] Schechter, S. (1982) *Op cit*. Footnote 92.

[303] Kelly, L. (1988) *Op cit*. Footnote 299.

[304] For example, HM Government (1997) *1997 Protection from Harassment Act*. www.legislation.gov.uk/ukpga/1997/40/contents [November 2016].

[305] Home Office (2015) *Controlling or Coercive Behaviour in an Intimate or Family Relationship Statutory Guidance Framework*. London, Home Office.

period of time. This approach is consistent with the methodology of 'violence against women' surveys that focus on counting victims and do not count the number of separate events. This means that even though there may be several violent actions spread over a period of time, these are counted as one. This produces a much lower count of violence than more traditional methods of separately counting events.

The alternative approach is to count each violent event – for example, crimes or health episodes – as well as the number of victims[306]. This approach is more consistent with conventional crime and health statistics.

Implications for measurement

Domestic violence encompasses several different forms of violence and coercion and is distinctively defined by the nature of the relationship between perpetrator and victim. The best approach to the measurement of domestic violence should follow the logic of this definition, seeking to identify all relevant forms of violence and whether the relationship between perpetrator and victim is a domestic one. The range of relevant forms of violence includes all those discussed in this chapter: physical violence (homicide and assault); sexual violence, including rape; FGM; forced sterilisation; stalking; harassment, forced marriage and – where relevant – trafficking in human beings. Repetition is important for the gender patterning of violence; data should be collected on this. The relationship between perpetrator and victim should differentiate between domestic relations (including between intimate partners and other family members) and acquaintances and strangers. Data on all gender dimensions should be collected, using all three measurement units of event, victim and perpetrator.

Gender mainstreaming (UN and EU policy), not gender invisibility (UNODC) or women only (UN Women), should be a principle of data collection. Data collection also needs to include all gender dimensions, not only the sex of the victim, in its mandatory categories.

---

[306]   Walby, S., Towers, J. and Francis, B. (2014) *Op cit.* Footnote 90.

Collecting data on women alone is not enough to ascertain the gendered patterns of domestic violence. Mainstreaming also requires the collection of data on the number of repetitions of violent events, since this repetition is deeply saturated with gender inequality.

Administrative data will always be insufficient for the measurement of the extent of domestic violence, since such a small proportion of cases are reported to the police and other agencies and that proportion is unknown. Only surveys can potentially measure the extent of domestic violence; this depends on the use of quality methodology (see next chapter). If this reaches an adequate quality threshold over time and across countries, then an indicator on the rate of domestic violence, by gender, would be possible.

Violence against women

Violence against women is named in the title of international legal instruments, including the UN *Declaration on the Elimination of Violence against Women* (DEVAW), the Council of Europe *Istanbul Convention on Preventing and Combating Violence against Women and Domestic Violence* and the *Inter-American Convention on the Prevention, Punishment and Eradication of Violence against Women 'Convention of Belem do Para'*. Thus, 'violence against women' is a category in international law; however, it is rarely used as a category in national criminal law. Violence against women is a category in public policy, especially at the level of the UN, including in the Sustainable Development Goals.

Hence, it is important to produce a measurement framework that is capable of delivering statistics and indicators on 'violence against women'. This requires the gender disaggregation of the sex of the victim of all forms of violence. While the approach of UN Women will deliver this, that of the UNODC does not. The UNODC could easily meet this requirement by changing the status of data collected on the sex of the victim from an optional tag to a mandatory field.

Conclusion

While different forms of violence are recognised in international as well as national law, they share many common features. Most of the features of the proposed measurement framework apply regardless of distinctions in the form of violence; nevertheless, these distinctions need to be respected where they produce relevant differences. The general features of the framework include events, victims and perpetrators, as well as the five gender dimensions: sex of victim; sex of perpetrator; relationship between perpetrator and victim; sexual aspect; and gender motivation. There are also general requirements for consistency in technical rules concerning 'non-completion' and counting.

For physical violence, in relation to homicide/femicide, it is possible to utilise data from administrative sources, especially the criminal justice system. However, there is missing data and there are some challenges in the consistent application of technical rules. For assault, the definitions used in different countries are inconsistent. For rape, there are definitions in use that are out of alignment with international law and much missing data. For other forms of violence, there needs to be careful attention to the definitions used in the framework and further work in developing data collection from both administrative sources and surveys.

With relatively small changes to measurement mechanisms, data, statistics and indicators could be produced for homicide/femicide and domestic violence. In the long term, the development of the measurement framework should enable the production of data, statistics and indicators on all forms of violence named in international law.

5
COLLECTING DATA

Introduction

Where can relevant data be found and collected? There are two main sources: administrative and survey. Data on violence against women and men is collected during administrative processes by public services, as well as by deliberate endeavour through social surveys conducted for academic researchers and governments. It is a challenge to ensure the use of a common set of definitions and units of measurement that facilitates cooperation among relevant entities and overcomes the current fragmentation and incompatibility between data collectors, while not neglecting the requirements of particular services.

Since the data is collected for a wide variety of purposes, it is unsurprising that a wide variety of definitions and units of measurement are currently used. This has suited the specific purposes of each of the many organisations involved. However, this diversity may mean disorganised fragmentation in relation to the larger picture of cooperation among multiple agencies to end violence. How is interagency cooperation to be achieved if each conceptualises and measures violence in a different way? How can they agree on whether violence is increasing or decreasing if they cannot agree on what counts as violence or the units in which to collect data? In order to ascertain whether violence is increasing or decreasing – for an individual, a group or a country – the collection of data within the same measurement framework is required. Further, surveys and public services that collect administrative data need to use the same measurement framework.

Yet, there are also specialised needs for information by different services and particular information that only specific services can discover. Some of these forms of knowledge can be useful to other agencies. Thus, while the need for a shared measurement framework on basics is essential, there is service specificity in information collection that is useful not only to the service gathering this data but also to other services engaged in mitigating and preventing violence. The aim in this chapter is to identify not only the data each service collects for its own purposes but also the data that may be used by others in the shared endeavour of ending violence. This may mean asking services to collect data that is relevant to other agencies with which it cooperates – even when it might not appear to have obvious relevance to their own immediate goals.

Whether the rate of violence is going up or down, or is more common in one location than another, is important information for decision-making by publics and policy makers as well as for research. 'Indicators' are condensations of complex data for use in these contexts. The priority interest for indicators concerns variations in the rate of violence in the population. Such indicators may also be included as part of other indicators, such as those on gender equality or sustainable development.

While survey data potentially provides a view of variations in violence in the population, administrative data usually provides a view of variations in service use. Variations in service use may better reflect changes in services provided than changes in the rate of violence. Rarely will variations in administrative data reflect variations in the real rate of violence. Collecting data relevant for indicators is thus very challenging. In administrative data, only homicide gets close to meeting this challenge. In surveys, data on the more frequent forms of violence could potentially be collected robustly.

This chapter investigates the best sources of data collection and remaining challenges. It examines data collection practices in the criminal justice system, health care, social services and specialised services, as well as surveys that collect data on violence against women and men.

ADMINSTRATIVE DATA

Introduction

Sources of administrative data include the agencies, authorities and services that engage with victims or perpetrators of violence: police; prosecutors; judiciary, health services, social services and specialised service providers.

Many public services focus on mitigating the harms of violence rather than preventing it. Thus, administrative data often concerns the consequences of violence rather than its nature or causes. Agencies treat injuries (health services), mitigate harms to bystanders such as children (social services) and offer refuge (specialised services). Only the criminal justice system is centrally concerned with the violence itself, as it addresses the actions and intentions of perpetrators. These different functions affect the data that services collect. Hence, in seeking to measure violence, more detailed attention is paid to the measurement activities of the criminal justice system (which is centred on perpetration of violence) than other services (which are centred on the mitigation of harms caused by the violence).

Multiple agencies need to cooperate if the goal of reducing violence is to be achieved. The use of the same measurement framework is necessary for the effective exchange of data that multiagency working requires. Although all European countries collect annual administrative statistics on violence and other crime[307], definitions, units of measurement and processes of data collection can vary between

---

[307]   Aebi, M. et al. (2014) *Op cit.* Footnote 193.

policy domains: criminal justice – especially police and judiciary[308] – health[309], social services[310] and specialised service provision[311]. Further, the administrative crime data for many forms of violence has restricted comparability between countries as a consequence of legal and policy variation.

The proposed measurement framework requires the following data to be collected:

• form of violence;

[308] Heiskanen, M., Aebi, M., van der Brugge, W. and Jehle, J.-M. (2014) *Recording Community Sanctions and Measures and Assessing Attrition: A Methodological Study on Comparative Data in Europe.* HEUNI Publication Series No. 77. Helsinki, Tammerprint Oy; Heiskanen, M. (2001) 'How to study sensitive topics', in Keeler, L. (ed.) *Recommendations of the E.U. Expert Meeting on Violence Against Women.* Ministry of Social Affairs and Health. Helsinki, Edita: 129–36; Francis, B., Hargreaves, C. and Soothill, K. (2015) 'Changing patterns of sex offender prevalence: disentangling age, year and generational effects over time', in Blokland, A and Lussier, P (eds) *Sex Offenders: A Criminal Career Approach.* Wiley, New York: 231–256; Corradi, C. and Stöckl, H. (2014) *Op cit.* Footnote 141; Kelly, L. (2005) *Research Review on Reporting, Investigation and Prosecution of Rape Cases.* London, HMCPSI; Kelly, L., Brown, H. and Westmorland, N. (2010) *Connections and Disconnections: Assessing Evidence, Knowledge and Practice in Relation to Rape.* London, Government Equalities Office; Walby, S. (2005) 'Improving the statistics on violence against women', *Statistical Journal of UNECE*, 22: 193–216.

[309] Olive, P. (2007) 'Care for emergency department patients who have experienced domestic violence: a review of the evidence base', *Journal of Clinical Nursing*, 16: 1736–48; Helelarsen, K. and Helweg-Larsen, K. (2013) 'Violence against women in Europe: magnitude and the mental health consequences described by different data sources', in Garcia-Moreno, C. and Riecher-Rössler, A. (eds) *Violence against Women and Mental Health: A Comprehensive Overview on the Psychological Sequelae of Violence against Women Worldwide.* Switzerland, Karger; Stöckl, H. (2014) 'Screening women for intimate partner violence: moving beyond screening for an adequate health care response to intimate partner violence', *Evidence-Based Medicine*, 19: 240.

[310] Palmer, E. (2012) 'Systematic and just: the use of a systematic review methodology in social work research', *Social Work and Social Science Review*, 15: 72–85.

[311] Balderston, S. (2012) 'After disablist hate crime: which interventions really work to resist victimhood and build resilience with survivors?' in Roulstone, A. and Mason-Bish, H. (eds) *Disability, Hate Crime and Violence.* London, Routledge; Towers, J. and Walby, S. (2012) *Measuring the Impact of Cuts in Public Expenditure on the Provision of Services to Prevent Violence Against Women and Girls.* London, Trust for London and Northern Rock Foundation.

- gender: the sex of the victim; the sex of the perpetrator; the relationship between perpetrator and victim: intimate partner or other family member, acquaintance or stranger; sexual aspect; gender motivation; sometimes also the location or setting of the violence;
- how many: three units of measurement – events, victims and perpetrators.

The improvement of administrative data collection is assisted by the analysis in several reviews, including the Council of Europe stocktaking study in 2006[312]; the Council of Europe study of administrative data relevant to violence against women[313]; the Council of Europe monitoring reports on the implementation of Recommendation Rec(2002)5[314]; the European Institute for Gender Equality (EIGE) study of administrative data[315]; the EIGE study of the provision of specialised services to victims in European Union (EU) Member States[316]; the Women Against Violence Europe (WAVE) report on specialist services[317]; and the European Commission review of relevant

[312] Council of Europe (2006) *Combating Violence against Women: Stocktaking Study on the Measures and Actions Taken in Council of Europe Member States.* Strasbourg, Council of Europe.

[313] Council of Europe (2008) *Administrative Data Collection on Domestic Violence in Council of Europe Member States.* Report authored by Ruuskanen, E. and Aromaa, K. EG-VEW-DC. www.coe.int/t/dg2/equality/domesticviolencecampaign/Source/EG-VAW-DC(2008)Study_en.pdf [November 2016].

[314] Council of Europe (2014) *Analytical Study of the Results of the Fourth Round of Monitoring the Implementation of Recommendation Rec(2002)5 on the Protection of Women Against Violence in Council of Europe Member States.* Report prepared by Hagemann-White, C. Strasbourg, Council of Europe Gender Equality Commission.

[315] EIGE (2014a) *Administrative Data Sources on Gender-Based Violence Against Women in the EU: Current Status and Potential for the Collection of Comparable Data.* http://eige.europa.eu/sites/default/files/MH0113492ENN_PDF.Web_.pdf [November 2016]; EIGE (2014b) *Administrative Data Sources on Gender-Based Violence Against Women in the EU: Online Mapping Tool.* http://eige.europa.eu/gender-based-violence/administrative-data-sources/about [November 2016].

[316] EIGE (2012) *Review of the Implementation of the Beijing Platform for Action in the EU Member States: Violence Against Women – Victim Support.* http://eige.europa.eu/sites/default/files/documents/Violence-against-Women-Victim-Support-Report.pdf [November 2016].

[317] Women Against Violence Europe (WAVE) (2015) *WAVE Report 2015 on the Role of Specialist Women's Support Services in Europe.* Vienna, WAVE.

EU legislation[318]. These reviews make various recommendations about the data to be collected by the various aforementioned agencies, which provide useful stepping stones towards harmonised data collection. For example, the Council of Europe study of administrative data collection on domestic violence recommended that – at a minimum – the police; the public prosecutor; the courts of first instance (both criminal and civil); the cause of death investigators, the healthcare services and the social services collect the following data: type of violence; sex of victim and perpetrator; age of victim and perpetrator; and relationship between victim and perpetrator (thus distinguishing cases of domestic violence from other cases).

Abstracting relevant data into national statistical systems goes beyond data collection. In some cases, while the relevant raw data is routinely collected, its abstraction into statistics at national level is less developed. For example, police files will almost always contain information, derived from interviews and statements during the investigation of an alleged crime, on the sex of the victim and alleged perpetrator and any relationship between them; but, in some countries, the sex of victim and perpetrator and their domestic or intimate relationship is not selected for inclusion during the process of abstracting information into the national statistical system. In this situation, the reform necessary to meet the recommended measurement framework does not require primary data collection but rather ensuring that the data selected from locally held files for inclusion in national summary statistics includes the important details. Implementing reforms to the abstracting system is much less expensive than reforming processes of primary data collection.

The levels of collecting and processing data include:

- Narrative handwritten record held locally;
- Narrative typed record held locally;
- Key abstracted information held locally in a computer-based system;

---

[318]   European Commission (2010) *Op cit.* Footnote 57.

- Key abstracted information in a computer-based system held nationally but not available to the public;
- Key abstracted information in a computer-based system held nationally and available to the public;
- Key abstracted information in a computer-based system available internationally and to the public.

Data held at the initial level is more detailed than that reported to the public at higher levels. Changing the priorities for the selection of data to be reported upwards may be relatively straightforward, especially since it may be treated as an addition rather than an alternative within the statistical system.

Administrative data concerns the extent of and manner in which services are used. This is important – but it does not necessarily reflect the underlying rate of violence in the population. Thus, administrative data may not indicate whether violence is increasing or decreasing, with one exception – homicide/femicide – discussed shortly.

Criminal justice system

The criminal justice system is an important source of administrative data on violence; most countries produce statistics on violent crime annually. However, there are challenges concerning consistent definitions and units of measurement to ensure comparability within different parts of the criminal justice system and between countries.

Two purposes of measurement exist: ascertaining changes in the real rate of violence and changes in the effective engagement of the agency. With the exception of homicide, most violent crimes are not reported to criminal justice authorities; there is thus an uncertain relationship between the numbers of crimes reported and the actual numbers of crimes in the population. The lack of robust relationship between the violence reported and the real rate of violence means that criminal justice data cannot be used to indicate the real rate of violence in the population, again with the exception of homicide. Nevertheless, the data is still useful in monitoring some aspects of the effectiveness of the criminal justice system; through the use of 'conviction rates', for example.

Homicide data is more robust and detailed than that on other forms of violent crime because most homicides come to the attention of the authorities. This means that if the rate of homicide reported to administrative authorities increases, it is likely that the real rate of homicide has increased. This is unlike other violent crimes, where a low proportion is reported and the relationship between the rate of reporting and the real rate in the population cannot be reliably estimated. Homicide data is usually collected by both criminal justice and health services, often with similar total numbers. In some cases, enough data is collected to enable distinctions between different forms, including incomplete acts and the five gender dimensions. However, data on gender of the perpetrator and the relation between the victim and the perpetrator is not routinely publicly available in many countries[319], although some European countries do have this information[320].

Conviction rates are a measure of the success of a criminal justice system in holding perpetrators of crimes to account. They require the number of criminals and the number of convictions. Since different parts of the criminal justice system use different units of measurement (the police measure crimes while courts measure perpetrators), this is challenging. The same unit of measurement is required throughout the criminal justice system to produce conviction rates.

The definitions of forms of violence that criminal justice authorities use vary between countries. For example, in some countries the threshold for physical assault is touch without consent that causes pain, while for others the threshold is higher and includes a visible

---

[319]   UNODC (2013) *Op cit.* Footnote 1.
[320]   Granath, S., Hagsted, J., Kivivuori, J., Lehti, M., Ganpat, S., Liem, M. and Nieuwbeerta, P. (2011) *Homicide in Finland, the Netherlands and Sweden: A First Study on the European Homicide Monitor Data.* Brå research reports 2011/15. Norstedts, Västerås; Lehti, M. (2015) *Henkirikoskatsaus 2015* ('Homicide Review 2015'). *Katsauksia 1/2015. Kriminologian ja oikeuspolitiikan instituutti.* Helsinki, Criminology and Justice Policy Institute.

injury before it is included in police-recorded crime statistics[321]. These variations in definition may be linked to variations in national laws. There are attempts to mitigate or otherwise address the consequences of variations in national criminal codes so as to achieve consistent measurement across countries, including the European Sourcebook project and the United Nations Office on Drugs and Crime (UNODC) International Classification of Crime for Statistical Purposes (ICCS).

The European Sourcebook project presents data on crime in Europe, paying careful attention to the differences in definitional and measurement practices. The fifth edition[322] collected data on violence (homicide, including attempts and completed homicide; bodily injury (assaults); aggravated bodily injury; sexual assault and rape; and sexual abuse of a child) from different levels of the criminal justice system (police; prosecution; courts, prison and alternative sanctions and measures). Because crime definitions in European countries differ, standard definitions were developed for each crime category. The standard definitions were supported by detailed instructions that guided the country correspondents in data collection, including what kind of incidents to include and exclude. The conclusion drawn here is that the use of detailed descriptions of behaviour rather than summary terms can be an important part of the process of ensuring that data is comparable between countries where international legal instruments do not provide sufficiently comparable definitions.

The ICCS is an initiative under the leadership of the UNODC and supported by the UN Statistics Commission[323]. It is intended to facilitate comparative analysis of crime between countries by constructing a single international classification. The framework is potentially relevant to the collection of data on violence against women and men, including homicide and domestic violence; it categorises crimes as either 'acts leading to harm or intending to cause harm to the person' or 'injurious acts of a sexual nature'. The ICCS attempts

---

[321] Aebi, M. et al. (2014) *Op cit.* Footnote193.
[322] Aebi, M. et al. (2014) *Op cit.* Footnote 193.
[323] UNODC (2015) *Op cit.* Footnote 33.

to avoid the problem of variations in legal definition of crimes by adopting a framework based on behaviour rather than legal category. It states that the priorities in making distinctions between categories are those that are most relevant to policy priorities. This classification addresses some of the detailed measurement issues, where the use of common standards is necessary to ensure comparability. This includes the threshold that distinguishes between violence and not-violence (including as it pertains to the concepts of force, coercion, threats, harm and without consent, which can vary between different forms of violence), the scaling of severity of violence and the significance of intentionality (especially important in relation to homicide). The ICCS is intended to be 'applicable for all forms of data on crime that are collected at different stages of the criminal justice process (police, prosecution, conviction, imprisonment) as well as in crime victimization surveys'[324].

The ICCS has a series of different 'levels' in its classification. Level 1 has 11 categories, the first three of which are relevant to the measurement framework: '1. Acts leading to death or intending to cause death, 2. Acts leading to harm or intending to cause harm to the person, 3. Injurious acts of a sexual nature[325]. This might therefore be considered a promising step towards a unified measurement framework. However, ICCS Version 1.0 does not adequately address the five gender dimensions; indeed, does not even address the first three, since it does not require the collection of data on the sex of the victim and perpetrator or the relationship between them. Sex of the victim and relationship between perpetrator and victim are merely optional tags in the current ICCS framework. Thus, it does not mandate the collection of data necessary to discover domestic violence, homicide of women, domestic homicide or violence against women.

In the next iteration of the ICCS, it would be straightforward to remedy this deficit by raising the status of sex of victim and perpetrator

---

[324]   UNODC (2015) *Op cit:* 5. Footnote 33.
[325]   UNODC (2015) *Op cit:* 325. Footnote 33.

and relationships between them (at least these three of the five gender dimensions) to mandatory categories, not optional tags.

Information on gender is uneven not only in new measurement mechanisms like the UNODC ICCS, but also in crime categories across the criminal justice system. In many jurisdictions, national statistics do not present data on the sex of victim and perpetrator or the relationship between them. Yet, in most criminal justice systems, police collect this information during their enquiries. Thus, consistency with the measurement framework does not require new and expensive data collection but rather reporting on the data collected and recorded in one part of the criminal justice system to others, including national published statistics.

The unit of measurement often varies between different parts of the criminal justice system; the police usually focus on crimes and prosecutors and courts usually focus on perpetrators. Both have been criticised for insufficient focus on victims. The solution is for each branch of the criminal justice system to use all three units of measurement: victims, crimes and perpetrators. The data is almost always collected in all three units (for example, the police will enquire about the number of victims, the number of crimes and the number of perpetrators), but is rarely abstracted for national statistical systems.

The Council of Europe Convention requires the study of conviction rates, which are an important indicator of the efficacy of the criminal justice system in relation to violence against women and domestic violence. Conviction rates measure the extent to which crimes reported to the criminal justice system lead to the conviction of their perpetrator. The Convention makes reference to the need to measure conviction rates in Article 11.1.*b*. Conviction rates can be constructed either for different parts of the criminal justice system (for example, only from the point of prosecution to conviction) or for the system as a whole (for example, comparing the number of crimes reported to surveys with the number of perpetrators convicted in the courts). While rates specific to particular sections of the criminal justice system are relevant for those sections, it is important to have conviction rates for the criminal justice system as a whole. In order to study conviction rates, it is necessary to have data that uses the same definitions and units of measurement from start to finish. If there are different definitions or units of measurement, it is hard – if not impossible – to find out how many 'cases' that enter the criminal justice system lead to conviction. It is thus important that the police, prosecutors, judiciary, courts and prisons and probation services all use the same definitions and units of measurement. Currently, many countries use different units at different stages of the criminal justice system: crimes (events, incidents) by the police and perpetrators (offenders, criminals) by the judiciary and prisons. (These often differ from specialised services, which use 'victims'). Those countries that currently use different units of measurement (victims, crimes, offenders) in different parts of the criminal justice system will need to bring these into alignment if they are to measure conviction rates effectively, as required by the Convention. They can do this either by selecting a single preferred measure throughout the criminal justice and court system or by requiring the collection of data using all three of the measurement units at each stage of the criminal justice system. Cooperation is more likely to be achieved by requiring the use of all three measurement units than trying to enforce collection in just one. For example, counting the number of victims, crimes and perpetrators at every stage is better than counting victims at one stage (for example, surveys), crimes at another (for example, police) and offenders at another (for example, courts).

Way forward: criminal justice system

The criminal justice system collects data on homicide that is potentially sufficiently robust to act as one indicator of violence against women and men. Homicide data is more reliable than that on the other forms of violence, which are systematically under-reported and recorded.

It would require further development work to collect comparative data from across criminal justice systems on physical assaults, rape and female genital mutilation (FGM), which would enable the construction of conviction rates to help monitor the effectiveness of the system.

A common definition should be used. The UNODC ICCS framework could form the basis of this, giving globally comparative data over time – but only if the next iteration makes data collection on the sex of the victim and perpetrator and the relationship between them mandatory.

Health system

Violence is a health issue, since it causes harms to wellbeing[326]. Health services are concerned with the mitigation of these harms. The classifications used in health focus on the injuries consequent on the violence. Less attention is paid in health to the consistent measurement of the nature of the violence and its perpetration (although this aspect is relevant to public health).

For the health service, violence is most often distinguished from not-violence by the harm suffered: the injury. The violent act and the harm suffered are analytically distinguished; the causal connection between them is treated as an issue that is the appropriate focus of ongoing research[327]. This approach is different to the criminal justice system, in which the act and the harm jointly and simultaneously contribute to the definition of the core categories.

---

[326]   Krug, E. et al. (2002) *Op cit*. Footnote 14; Violence Prevention Alliance (2015)
The Public Health Approach. Geneva, WHO; WHO (2014) *Op cit*. Footnote 14.

[327]   WHO (2013) *Global and Regional Estimates of Violence against Women: Prevalence and Health Effects of Intimate Partner Violence and Non-Partner Sexual Violence*. Geneva, WHO; Black, M., Basile, K., Breiding, M., Smith, S., Walters, M., Merrick, M., Chen, J. and Stevens, M. (2011) *The National Intimate Partner and Sexual Violence Survey (NISVS): 2010 Summary Report*. Atlanta, National Centre for Injury Prevention and Control, Centres for Disease Control and Prevention; Devries, K., Mak, J., Bacchus, L., Child, J., Falder, G., Petzold, M., Astbury, J. and Watts, C. (2013) 'Intimate partner violence and incident depressive symptoms and suicide attempts: a systematic review of longitudinal studies', *PLOS Medicine Open Access*, doi: 10.1371/journal.pmed.1001439; Vos, T., Astbury, J., Piers, L., Magnus, A., Heenan, M., Stanley, L., Walker, I. and Webster, K. (2006) 'Measuring the impact of intimate partner violence on the health of women in Victoria, Australia', *Bulletin of the World Health Organisation*, 84: 739–44; Campbell, J. (2002) 'Health consequences of intimate partner violence', *The Lancet*, 359: 1331–6.

Health focuses on the event, since healthcare is usually delivered in discrete episodes to the victim who is harmed, although potentially event-based data could be analysed with a focus on the victim. Data about the perpetrator is rarely collected in health systems. The gender dimension of harm is not a primary concern to health practitioners, though information about the sex of the victim is often available from linked datasets.

The World Health Organization (WHO) International Classification of Diseases (ICD) framework is the leading global classification of disease and health problems. Shorter, reduced forms of the ICD are used in particular settings; for example, the International Shortlist for Hospital Morbidity Tabulation (ISHMT). The ICD[328] has several classifications for 'intentional injury'. 'Assault' is the ICD's category frame for 'injuries inflicted by another person with intent to injure or kill, by any means'[329]. There are multiple subcategories of forms of assault (X85–Y09), sub-classified into injury causing objects (for example, handgun) or modes of violent action (for example, strangulation). The category of 'sexual assault' (Y05) is defined in the ICD as sexual assault by bodily force[330]. The category of 'assault' is used in several health measurement frameworks affiliated with the ICD, including the International Classification of External Causes of Injury (ICECI)[331] and Injury Surveillance Guideline (ISG). Within the category of 'assault', intentionality of the violence is explicit. Multiple actors implement the ICD in different sites across health systems; the framework is open to implementation in ways that have led to significant variation in the depth of data collected.

In individual health systems, other data collection frameworks are utilised in conjunction with or instead of the ICD. For example, in England, emergency departments' data collection categories are set

---

[328] WHO (2016) *International Classification of Diseases ICD-10 Version 2016 Assault (X85–Y09)*. Geneva, WHO.

[329] WHO (2016) *Op cit*. Footnote 328.

[330] WHO (2016) *Op cit*. Footnote 328.

[331] WHO (2004) *International Classification of External Causes of Injury (ICECI) Version 1.2*. Geneva, WHO.

by the Standardisation Committee for Care Information (SCCI)[332]. Here, too, 'assault' is one of the categories for cause of injury[333]. Sexual assault is currently not a discrete category, though this is proposed in a new emergency care dataset under development[334].

Data is also collected in more detailed patient notes (similar to the more detailed data recorded in notebooks by police officers at the scene), which are held locally. Descriptors of acts of the physical violence (punched, hit, dragged and so on) perpetrated by intimate partners were found to be recorded more frequently in narrative records than inputted in the more formal computer-based administrative data collection system[335]. This is likely because an act of violence, as a mechanism of injury, is important clinical information that can signal potential physical injury risk. Thus, like criminal justice systems, the necessary data is often collected in some parts of the system but is not routinely extracted into the formal statistical systems.

In health settings, the sex of the person injured or harmed is routinely collected at the local level but this data is not necessarily forwarded to national systems. A study on administrative data sources on gender-based violence in the EU indicated that data of the sex of the person subjected to interpersonal violence at state level was possible for just ten EU Member States[336]. There is also variation in the reporting of the sex of the victim by different types of health services. For example, in England, inpatient assault data are disaggregated by sex[337] but

---

332   NHS Digital (2016) *Information Standards and Collections (Including Extractions)*. http://content.digital.nhs.uk/isce.

333   Olive, P. (2013) *Classifications of Intimate Partner Violence in Hospital Based Emergency Department Health Systems*. Lancaster, Lancaster University [unpublished thesis]; NHS Digital (2016) *Accident and Emergency Department Commissioning Dataset*. www.datadictionary.nhs.uk/data_dictionary/messages/cds_v6-2/data_sets/cds_v6-2_type_010_-_accident_and_emergency_cds_fr.asp?shownav=1 [November 2016].

334   NHS England (2016) *Emergency Care Data Set* (ECDS). www.england.nhs.uk/ourwork/tsd/ec-data-set/ [November 2016].

335   Olive, P. (2013) *Op cit*. Footnote 333.

336   EIGE (2016) *Administrative Data Sources on GBV in the EU, Types of GBV and Sectors*. Vilnius, EIGE.

337   NHS Digital (2016) *Assaults April 2013, March 2014*. http://content.digital.nhs.uk/media/14753/Assaults-April-2013-March-2014/pdf/Assaults_April_2013_March_2014.pdf [November 2016].

emergency department assault data are not[338]. Thus, a person's sex is likely to be routinely recorded when healthcare is accessed, but the extent to which this data is then captured and published by national systems is more varied. As the data is captured at some point in the administrative process, it is not necessary to extend the categories for data collection, but rather to ensure that the already collected data on the sex of the victim is mandatorily extracted into national, regional and global systems to ensure consistent application of the full measurement framework.

Information about the sex of the perpetrator is not routinely recorded in either the narrative local health records or in national administrative health systems[339]. For example, the sex of the perpetrator is not a category in WHO's ISG, even at the supplementary optional data level. However, specialised sexual violence health services, such as SARCs (Sexual Assault Referral Centres) in the UK, do record information about perpetrators. This suggests that it would be possible to include the sex of the perpetrator in health data systems.

A category of victim–perpetrator relationship exists in health measurement frameworks such as ISG and ICECI, but because of its designation as optional, data is not reliably collected on this. One major challenge to the collection of this data in health systems is the implication for criminal justice procedures if a perpetrator is identified. The victim–perpetrator relationship may be captured locally; for example, one study found that a victim–perpetrator relationship had been documented by practitioners in two thirds (68%) of narrative emergency department health records[340] though this is not usually abstracted into national systems. In England, victim–perpetrator

---

[338] NHS Digital (2016) *Accident and Emergency Attendances in England 2014–15*. http://content.digital.nhs.uk searchcatalogue?productid=20143&q=title%3a%22accident+and+emergency +attendances%22&topics= 0%2fHospital+care&sort=Relevance&size=10&pag e=1#top [November 2016].

[339] Olive, P. (2013) *Op cit*. Footnote 333; EIGE (2014a) *Op cit*. Footnote 315.

[340] Olive, P. (2013) *Op cit*. Footnote 333.

relationship data is not mandated in data systems[341] and a report shows this was possible for only four EU Member States[342].

Most of the categories of physical assault in the ICD-10 are not classified by the victim–perpetrator relationship. The few ICD-10 assault categories in which this is possible are 'T74.1 Maltreatment Syndrome' caused by physical partner abuse, 'Y06.0 Neglect and Abandonment by a partner' and 'Y07.0 Assault / Maltreatment (Mental cruelty, physical abuse, sexual abuse, torture) by a partner', though there are a number of shortcomings even with these categories[343].

The location of violence is included in measurement frameworks in health and the data is used in analyses informing public policy on community safety[344]. The 'domestic' location has been used as a proxy for victim–perpetrator relationship where this data is not directly available, even though it is not exactly the same.

The unit of measurement in health services is principally episode-based. This aligns well with other event-based measurement frameworks, such as police-recorded crime. Data is less often published by victim and rarely if ever by perpetrator. However, since many health services use unique person identifiers, patients' records could potentially be used to create statistics centred on the victim.

[341] Olive, P. (2013) *Op cit.* Footnote 333; NHS Digital (2016) *Op cit.* Footnote 338.
[342] Walby, S. and Olive, P. (2013) *Estimating the Costs of Gender-Based Violence in the European Union.* Luxembourg, Publications Office of the European Union.
[343] Olive, P. (2013) *Op cit.* Footnote 334.
[344] Florence, C., Shepherd, J., Brennan, I. and Simon, T. (2011) 'Effectiveness of anonymised information sharing and use in health service, police and local government partnership for preventing violence related injury: experimental study and time series analysis', *British Medical Journal*, 342, doi: doi.10.1136/bmj. d3313 ; Quigg, Z., Hughes, K. and Bellis, M. (2012) 'Data sharing for prevention: a case study in the development of a comprehensive emergency department injury surveillance system and its use in preventing violence and alcohol related harms', *Injury Prevention*, 18: 315–20; Sivarajasingam, V., Page, N., Morgan, P. Matthews, K., Moore, S. and Shepherd, J. (2014) 'Trends in community violence in England and Wales 2005–2009', *Injury: International Journal of the Care of the Injured*, 45: 592–8.

Data is recorded by different actors, at different locations, for different purposes across health. More recently, datasets are being developed to record prevalence and health problems related to FGM[345].

Data may be held in an individual's medical record and be partially aggregated at local, national and international levels. A person's medical record, created at the point of service delivery, is often comprehensive and detailed; it may be handwritten and/or electronically stored. The data that is aggregated is more partial, responding to requirements of government, service commissioners and monitoring organisations.

It is possible to identify four levels: narrative records held locally; abstracted information held locally in a computer-based system; abstracted information in a computer-based system held nationally but not available to the public; and abstracted information in a computer based-system held nationally and available to the public. Health data concerning violence variously reaches these levels. Narrative records held locally likely hold most of the victim-centred information for the measurement framework. The key abstracted data category missing from local and national computer-based systems is perpetrator–victim relationship. Though this may be detailed in narrative records held locally, additional perpetrator information – such as age and sex of the perpetrator – is most commonly not measured at any level. Incident-based data of physical assaults is publicly available via the internet. For inpatient hospital episode statistics, the number of incidents of physical assaults is disaggregated by gender.

The use of unique identifiers (IDs) of individuals in most health services, including the National Health Service (NHS) in England, means it would be possible to collate and make public the number of victims – but this is rarely done. The use of such IDs means it is potentially possible to link data from health services with that from other public services. Such data linkage is achieved in the Nordic

---

[345]   NHS Digital (2016) *Female Genital Mutilation Datasets*. http://content.digital.nhs.uk/fgm [November 2016].

countries, such as Denmark, facilitating research that enables the long-term consequences of violence to be discovered[346].

Way forward: health system

Health systems do not yet provide reliable or comparable data on violence against women and men. This is partly because their main focus is the consequences of the violence rather than its nature and causation. Yet, the core components of the measurement framework could still be usefully used: the form of the violence (including physical assault and sexual assault); sex of victim and perpetrator; and the perpetrator–victim relationship; additionally, the location of the violence. The unit of measurement should be events, victims and (where possible) perpetrators. Many of these categories are already frequently recorded in narrative, locally-held records. The collection of data varies in depth and detail in different health locations, from handwritten narrative accounts with uneven but rich information through various processes of coding and abstraction to thinner data in national computerised systems. The local collection of detailed data offers the potential for significant enhancement of computerised health data at national and international levels if it were to be systematically coded and analysed.

Social services

Social services are concerned with 'safeguarding', which means attempting to prevent the re-occurrence of behaviours and vulnerabilities that led to harm. The focus is on safeguarding children as victims or as witnesses of violence in a family context; violence

---

[346] Helweg-Larsen, K. (2010) *Violence in Close Relationships: the Prevalence, Nature and Development and the National Efforts to Combat Partner Violence among Women and Men*. Copenhagen, National Institute of Public Health and Ministry of Gender Equality; Kruse, M., Sørensen, J., Brønnum-Hanse, H. and Helweg-Larsen, K. (2010) 'Identifying victims of violence using register-based data', *Scandinavian Journal of Public Health*, 36(6): 611–617.

against adults is rarely a focus for social services. There is some concern when domestic violence affects adults in situations of additional vulnerability, such as those associated with disability and FGM. There is little involvement in femicide or rape (other than of children)[347] and little concern with perpetrators.

This primary concern with safeguarding structures data collection: little data is collected on victims or perpetrators of violence, or on their relationship, unless the 'victim' is a child who has been subject to violence or witnessed violence against an adult in their family. When violence is recorded, this is cautious and vague and scales of severity are not used. However, the development of multiagency working requires the sharing of information, which raises the issue of developing the comparable data recommended in the proposed measurement framework.

Domestic violence is not screened for in social work assessments in England and Wales; in the UK, there is no requirement for mandatory reporting of domestic violence. In countries where this occurs, it is usually linked to the requirement to report child abuse[348] or child protection concerns[349].

FGM is a recent focus for action across the EU. For example, in the UK, the Serious Crime Act 2015 places a duty on professionals to report FGM in those under 18, where it has been either 'visually confirmed' or disclosure made by a young person. Failure to report suspected FGM will result in fitness to practice enquiries by the Health Care Professions Council, the regulatory body for social work in England[350].

While social work is an example of professional practice that is light in data, there are some attempts to gather this. The Child In Need

---

[347] McMahon, S. and Schwartz, R. (2011) 'A review of rape in the social work literature: a call to action', *Affilia*, 26: 250–63.

[348] Panaiotopoulos, C. (2011) 'Mandatory reporting of domestic violence cases in Cyprus: barriers to the effectiveness of mandatory reporting and issues for future practice', *European Journal of Social Work*, 14: 379–402.

[349] Humphreys, C. (2008) 'Problems in the system of mandatory reporting of children living with domestic violence', *Journal of Family Studies*, 14: 228–39.

[350] Home Office (2015) *Op cit.* Footnote 257.

(CIN) census records reasons for initial contact and assessment; in the CIN, abuse and neglect – which includes children at risk of domestic violence – is the most frequently noted category at 49.4%[351]. The CIN also collects case closure data on: '3A Domestic violence: Concerns about the child being the subject of domestic violence. 3B Domestic violence: Concerns about the child's parent/carer being the subject of domestic violence. 3C Domestic violence: Concerns about another person living in the household being the subject of domestic violence.'

Gender is not considered to be a significant category and thus data is rarely collected on (even) the sex of the victim. This is sometimes justified in the name of gender neutrality[352]; but this defence has been subject to much critique[353].

The narrative component of recording in case files might potentially allow for the mining of relevant data; however, this would require the use of concepts and categories in social work professional practice that are not currently deployed.

Way forward: social services

Many challenges exist to the contribution by social services to data collection on violence against women and men, including children. The current purpose of social services does not align with the identification of victims or perpetrators of violence, unless children are victims.

The requirement on social services to engage in multiagency working in cooperation with other public agencies – including the

---

[351] Department for Education (2015) *Children in Need Census: Additional Guidance on the Factors Identified at the End of Assessment.* London, HM Government.

[352] Coy, M. (2015) 'Working paper on intervention against domestic violence in England and Wales', from research project *Cultural Encounters in Intervention against Violence* (CEINAV), January 2015. http://www.londonmet.ac.uk/media/london-metropolitan-university/london-met-documents/faculties/faculty-of-social-sciences-and-humanities/research/child-and-woman-abuse-studies-unit/ceinav/DV-working-paper-UK-final-BG.pdf [November 2016].

[353] Hicks, S. (2015) 'Social work and gender: an argument for practical accounts,' *Qualitative Social Work*, 14: 471–87.

police and courts – is potentially a driver of change, since there is a need to develop meaningful and robust ways to share information. Such sharing requires a common measurement framework.

Specialised victim services

Specialised victim services offer expert victim-centred assistance to those who have suffered violence. They range from broad services for all victims of crime – for example, UK Victim Support – to highly specialised services offering bespoke care and counselling for particular forms of violence – for example, Rape Crisis Centres – with many in between that offer a focused range of specialised services, such as refuges/shelters, advice and advocacy. They may offer assistance centred on a building, such as refuges/shelters and SARCs, or they may be dispersed in mobile advisers, phone lines or websites. In addition to offering direct assistance to victims, they develop knowledge and expertise on the experiences of victims that can inform public debate, research and policy development. There are several reviews of such services[354].

Data collected by the specialised services include accounts of the experience of violence and associated circumstances in narrative and/ or summary forms, as well as provider-specific information about service use and outcomes. Potentially, specialised services could offer a unique contribution to knowledge on violence in longitudinal data, centred on the history of the experience of the victims. They have the potential to follow the victim's 'journey' through violence and service use in a way no other data collector could achieve.

Currently, each specialised service provider has its own bespoke measurement framework. These may extend across the several types of services that the provider offers (for example, both refuges and advisers). They include specialised instruments to collect information

---

[354] WAVE (2015) *Op cit.* Footnote 317; EIGE (2012) *Op cit.* Footnote 316; Coy, M., Kelly, L. and Foord, J. (2009) *Map of Gaps 2: The Postcode Lottery Of Violence Against Women Support Services.* London, EVAW and Equality and Human Rights Commission (EHRC); Towers, J. and Walby, S. (2012*) Op cit.* Footnote 311.

relevant to proprietary risk assessment tools, useful to other agencies such as the police.

When information is collected in narrative accounts, it is likely to include the full range of information recommended in our proposed measurement framework. However, the forms used to summarise the data input into computer systems and aggregated at organisational and national levels contain only a subset of this data. In particular, the unit of measurement is the victim rather than the event, so the data on the history of events is usually severely truncated. Further, the definition of violence is often loose, with unclear boundaries to concepts; it usually does not map directly onto legal categories. It is thus difficult to share or deploy this information in conjunction with other agencies and researchers.

Way forward: specialised services

If a common measurement framework were to be used, the data from specialised providers could be much more effectively deployed. The potential for collection and analysis of longitudinal data on the history of violence, associated circumstances and service use is under development by some specialised providers, but is limited by its lack of compatibility with police, prosecutors, courts, social services and other service providers, as well as lack of resourcing.

Ways forward: all administrative sources

Administrative data is routinely collected by agencies the victims of violence come into contact with as they seek justice, medical care, counselling, housing or other support. All agencies that assist victims of violence against women and men – including homicide, domestic violence, rape and FGM – should collect relevant data consistent with a shared measurement framework. This is necessary to develop the knowledge base for the improvement of each of these services, as well as for their collaborative and interagency work towards ending violence.

A modification of the current version of the ICCS is required so that the collection of data on the sex of victim and perpetrator and the relationship between them is mandatory, not optional. Data collected under this modified system would then enable, for example, comparisons of conviction rates for violent crimes across different countries and over time.

Only data on homicide is sufficiently reliable for use in an indicator on changes in violence; other forms of violence are infrequently and unevenly reported to the authorities, so an increase in reported rates is not a reliable indicator of the underlying rate of violence.

Surveys

Surveys are important sources of data on violence against women and men; since the majority of victims do not seek help from agencies and therefore are not included in administrative statistics, surveys are the best way of obtaining data on them.

With the exception of homicide, surveys are the only reliable way of discovering if the rate of violence is going up or down. This is because changes in the rate of those seeking assistance from authorities may reflect changes in the willingness of victims to approach the authorities and that of authorities to record help-seeking, rather than changes in the 'real' rate of violence. This also makes survey data the most reliable source for populating indicators on the scale of different forms of violence, for cross-national comparisons and change over time. Surveys additionally collect demographic and socioeconomic data on respondents; thus, survey data is not only important for measuring progress, but also needed to support theory testing and development on the causes and consequences of violence against women and men.

The purpose of early surveys was to identify the scale of the problem and raise awareness of it. More recently, the purpose has become more ambitious: to measure change and to compare the outcomes of different policy regimes. The Council of Europe's *Istanbul Convention* requires that Parties should 'endeavour to conduct population-based surveys at regular intervals to assess the prevalence of and trends in all forms of violence covered by the scope of this Convention' (Article 11.2). The ambition to measure change is also included in EU strategies.

Forms of violence

Surveys measuring violence against women and men should conform to the definition of violence established in Chapter Three and include all the forms of violence laid out in Chapter Four – with the exception of homicide/femicide, which cannot be collected in victimisation surveys and has not been routinely collected in perpetrator surveys.

Physical assault is the most prevalent form of violence, both across different countries and over time. Each survey of violence against women and men needs an adequate sample size to robustly capture physical assault disaggregated by at least two of the five gender dimensions: sex of the victim and all four types of relationship between perpetrator and victim (current or ex-intimate partners, other domestic relationship, acquaintance or stranger).

Where particular forms of violence are rare in specific contexts, a single survey will not robustly measure them because the sample size required would be prohibitively large. Nevertheless, all forms are relevant and should be routinely included in surveys of violence against women and men, even if this entails aggregating them within larger categories when reporting findings. This is necessary to ensure the survey instrument is relevant to the widest possible range of communities and countries and to enable the periodic reporting of rarer forms of violence aggregated across a number of years.

Gender

The survey should collect data and present findings on the five gender dimensions (see Chapter Three): sex of the victim; sex of the perpetrator; relationship between perpetrator and victim (current or ex-intimate partner, other domestic relationship, acquaintance or stranger); whether the violence has a sexual element (beyond the specific forms of rape and sexual assault); and whether there is a gender motivation to the violence. It would also be useful to collect data on the location or setting of the violence.

Survey models

There has been much innovation in surveys that measure violence, including reviews of the best ways to carry out a survey in order to generate relevant statistics and indicators, recommendations to improve survey methodology[355] and manuals offering practical guidance on the technical aspects[356].

Two main survey models for collecting data on violence have emerged: generic crime and health surveys, and violence against women surveys.

The generic surveys on crime or health started in the 1970s and are often still running today; For example, the Crime Survey for England and Wales (CSEW) (since 1982[357]), Denmark National Health Interview Surveys (since 2000[358]) and the USA National Crime Victimization Survey (since 1972[359]). These surveys typically collect data on the sex of the victim and the relationship between perpetrator and victim; some also ask about the sex of the perpetrator, but less

[355] Walby, S. and Myhill, A. (2001) 'New survey methodologies in researching violence against women', *British Journal of Criminology*, 41: 502–22; Walby, S. (2005) 'Improving the statistics on violence against women', *Statistical Journal of the United Nations Economic Commission for Europe*, 22: 193–216; UN Economic and Social Council (2006) *Violence against Women: Analysis of National Surveys Carried Out by Countries of the Conference of the European Statisticians to Measure Violence against Women*. Economic Commission for Europe Conference of European Statisticians, Group of Experts on Gender Statistics, 4th Session, Geneva, 11–13 September 2006; Walby, S., Towers, J. and Francis, B. (2014) *Op cit*. Footnote 90.

[356] UN Department for Economic and Social Affairs (2014) *Op cit*. Footnote 44.

[357] Walby, S. and Allen, J. (2004) *Op cit*. Footnote 81; Walby, S., Towers, J. and Francis, B. (2014) *Op cit*. Footnote 90; Walby, S., Towers, J. and Francis, B. (2016) *Op cit*. Footnote 6.

[358] Helweg-Larsen, K. (2010) *Op cit*. Footnote 346.

[359] Bureau of Justice Statistics. *National Crime Victimization Survey*. www.bjs.gov/index.cfm?ty=dcdetail&iid=245 [November 2016]; Truman, J. and Langton, L. (2015) *Criminal Victimization, 2014*. US Department of Justice, NCJ, 2489731. www.bjs.gov/content/pub/pdf/cv14.pdf [November 2016].

routinely. However, the official analysis of the collected data and the production of headline statistics and official indicators often aggregate (rather than disaggregate) the data, so the statistics and indicators produced are non-gendered; that is, gender is not visible. For example, the CSEW publishes statistics on different forms of violent crime that are not disaggregated by the sex of the victim, although the Swedish Crime Survey[360] does disaggregate. The CSEW does publish statistics on domestic violence, but not disaggregated by the sex of the victim.

These generic surveys typically use crime codes or health codes as definitional categories of violence for data collection. These provide data on the injury or other harm to health, as well as − in the case of crime codes − on the act, injury or other harm to health and the intention. Thus, severity can be established. The use of crime or health codes also means the data collected in generic crime and health surveys is comparable with administrative statistics.

While the most important data for gendering violence is typically collected, in particular the sex of the victim and the relationship between perpetrator and victim, the data that would deepen the understanding of the gendered nature of violence is less often collected; that is, the sex of the perpetrator, whether the violence contained a sexual element and whether there was a gender motivation.

The main development required in this survey model is changes in the analysis practices rather than in data collection principles, although expanding data collection to include all five gender dimensions is important in the longer term.

The invisibility of women's experiences of violence in official statistics was identified as in urgent need of address; thus, from the 1990s, specific and specialised violence against women surveys were developed. One of the first major surveys of violence against women was by Statistics Canada[361]. This was followed by a number of other

---

[360] Swedish Crime Survey [*Nationella trygghetsundersökningen (NTU)*] (2015). www. bra.se/bra/brott-och-statistik/statistik/utsatthet-for-brott/ntu.html [November 2016].

[361] Johnson, H. (1996) *Dangerous Domains: Violence against Women in Canada*. Canada, Nelson Canada.

specialist surveys, including the International Violence against Women Survey (IVAWS), conducted in 11 countries[362]; the WHO Multi-Country Study on Women's Health and Domestic Violence against Women, focusing on developing countries[363], the EU Fundamental Rights Agency (FRA) Violence against Women Survey[364] and country-specific specialised surveys, including 21 Member States of the Council of Europe that have carried out a representative national survey focusing on the prevalence of violence against women. Some specialist violence against women surveys have been repeated; for example, in the Czech Republic and Finland[365]; Italy plans to repeat its violence against women survey every 4 years[366]; in the US, a new ongoing National Intimate Partner and Sexual Violence Survey was launched in 2010, with baseline data published in 2014[367]. In some cases there have been specialised modules attached to larger health surveys, including in the Global South; for example, the Health and

[362] Johnson, H., Ollus, N. and Nevala. S. (2008) *Violence against Women: An International Perspective*. New York, Springer; Ollus, N., Johnson, H., Alvazzi del Frate, A. and Nevala, S. (2003) *Manual: International Violence against Women Survey* (unpublished). The research package including the interview questionnaire, methodological recommendations and detailed instructions on how to carry out the survey in an individual country is available from HEUNI; HEUNI (2013) *International Violence Against Women Survey*. www.heuni.fi/en/index/researchareas/violenceagainstwomen/internationalviolenceagainstwomensurveyivaws.html [November 2016].

[363] García-Moreno, C., Jansen, H., Ellsberg, M., Heise, L. and Watts, C. (2005) *WHO Multi-Country Study on Women's Health and Domestic Violence against Women: Initial Results on Prevalence, Health Outcomes and Women's Responses*. Geneva, WHO; WHO (2005) *Op cit*. Footnote.

[364] FRA (2014) *Op cit*. Footnote 92.

[365] Council of Europe (2014) *Monitoring of Recommendation Rec(2002)5 of the Committee of Ministers to Member States on the Protection of Women against Violence*. http://www.coe.int/t/dg2/equality/domesticviolencecampaign/Source/CDEG%20(2008)%20rev_en.pdf [November 2016].

[366] Maria Giuseppina Muratore, 'Data collection on violence against women and domestic violence', Council of Europe Conference on Data Collection, Kyiv, Ukraine, 3–4 September 2015. http://www.coe.int/en/web/stop-violence-against-women-ukraine/conference-on-data-collection [November 2016].

[367] Breiding, M., Smith, S., Basile, K., Walters, M., Chen, J. and Merrick, M. (2014) 'Prevalence and characteristics of sexual violence, stalking and intimate partner violence victimization: National Intimate Partner and Sexual Violence Survey, Unites States, 2011', *Surveillance Summaries*, 63(SS08): 1–18.

Demographic Surveys [368] have included modules on domestic violence and FGM[369].

This second survey model sought to address the invisibility of violence against women; as such, it focused on surveying women only, developing survey methodologies for violence against women and collecting data on the specific forms of violence to which women were disproportionately victim. For example, the surveys avoided stigmatised terms for violence and avoided screening questions that limited opportunities for women to disclose. Thus, some aspects of the gendered context of the violence are better addressed in specialist surveys than generic crime and health surveys. The sex of the perpetrator is often collected, along with other relevant data on the gender context of the violence. The sex of the victim does not need to be collected in the survey because the sampling frame includes only women (or women and girls, depending on the lower age limit).

Most of the specialised violence against women surveys use a modified version of the Conflict Tactics Scale (CTS), including FRA's EU-wide survey[370], the International Violence against Women survey[371] and national-level surveys, such as Germany's 'Health, Well-Being and Personal Safety of Women in Germany'[372] and the CSEW specialist Intimate Violence module[373]. The CTS defines violence by the act only, rather than requiring injury or other harm to health or the intention of the perpetrator. Even when this data is additionally collected, information on harms and intentions are not part of the definition of the core category used in the CTS. Thus, it does not meet the definition of crime in international law. Data collected using

---

[368] The Demographic and Health Survey Program. http://dhsprogram.com/What-We-Do/Survey-Types/DHS.cfm [November 2016]

[369] Termed 'Female Genital Cutting' in the survey module.

[370] FRA (2014) *Op cit.* Footnote 68.

[371] Johnson, H., Ollus, N. and Nevala, S. (2008) *Op cit.* Footnote 293.

[372] Federal Ministry for Family Affairs, Senior Citizens, Women and Youth (2004) *Health, Well-Being and Personal Safety of Women in Germany: A Representative Study of Violence against Women in Germany.* www.cahrv.uni-osnabrueck.de/conference/SummaryGermanVAWstudy.pdf [November 2016].

[373] Johnson, H. (2015) *Op cit.* Footnote 23.

the CTS is not comparable with data in criminal justice statistics, including the ICCS.

In order to collect the data needed for the proposed framework, this survey model requires widening the sampling frame to include both women and men and replacing the CTS with categories that are able to capture act, injury or other harms to health and intention. The use of crime codes in generic crime surveys has proven to be successful, providing data is collected on the sex of victim and perpetrator, the relationship between them and the gender context.

There are further surveys of specific populations. For example, the development of screening for domestic violence in health settings shares some of the characteristics of a survey, though not all are convinced of its effectiveness and appropriateness[374].

Developing the survey model

The development of a new survey model, which builds on the innovation and development of the two current models and addresses the key challenges for collecting and analysing data using surveys under our proposed measurement framework, is the focus of the rest of this section. Having addressed definitions of violence and gender, the remaining key challenges are:

- *Units of measurement*: events, victims and perpetrators.
- *Sampling frame*: representative of the population, reducing the exclusion of those groups most vulnerable to violence.
- *Method of survey delivery*: consistency over time and between countries, as well as confidentiality.
- *Question framing*: avoidance of stigmatising terminology and use of detailed description in which respondent can recognise their own experiences of violence.

---

[374]   Ramsay, J., Richardson, J., Carter, Y., Davidson, L. and Feder, G. (2002) 'Should health professionals screen women for domestic violence? Systematic review', *British Medical Journal*, 325: 314.

Units of measurement

Three units of measurement need to be consistently used for collecting data on all forms of violence in surveys: events, victims and perpetrators. Each is pertinent to the theorisation and interrogation of changes in the scale and form of violence across countries and over time. In particular, the number of events is always necessary, because violence by current or ex-intimate partners and other domestic relations is characterised by repeated attacks by the same perpetrator against the same victim[375]. It is necessary to identify the number of events per victim of different forms of crime, as well as the number of different forms of crime by different types of perpetrator, in order to identify if certain groups in the population are subject to alternative trajectories – and thus whether there are different causes and consequences for different forms of violence and different groups of victims and perpetrators. A number of analyses of crime survey data have found differences in the scale and trajectories of different forms of violence depending on whether the unit of measurement is victims or events[376].

Generic crime and health surveys typically use events (the number of crimes or episodes). Violence against women surveys typically use victims. Perpetrators are rarely the primary unit of measurement in surveys, although one example of a survey of rape perpetrators is that conducted by Jewkes et al. in South Africa[377]. This survey collected data from a representative sample of men aged 18–49 in two districts in South Africa, using the census as the primary sampling framework. It collected data on the sex (women and men) and age (adult or child) of the victim and their relationship with the rapist, including

[375] Farrell, G., Phillips, C. and Pease, K. (1995) 'Like Taking Candy', *British Journal of Criminology*, 35: 384–99.
[376] Walby, S., Towers, J. and Francis, B. (2016) *Op cit.* Footnote 6; Farrell, G. and Pease, K. (2010), 'The sting in the tail of the British Crime Survey', in Hough, M. and Maxfield, M. (eds) *Crime in the Twenty-First Century.* Boulder, Lynne Rienner Publishers: 33–53; Farrell, G., Philips, C. and Pease, K. (1995) *Op cit.* Footnote 375.
[377] See, for example, Jewkes, R., Sikweyita, Y., Morrell, R. and Dunkle, K. (2010) 'Why, when and how men rape: understanding rape perpetration in South Africa', *SA Crime Quarterly*, 34: 23–31.

current or ex-intimate partner, family, acquaintance or stranger. This survey also collected data on the motivation of the men who raped, identifying sexual entitlement as the most common reason, followed by entertainment and punishment.

The different survey models have collected data on the number of events, victims and perpetrators, but not always consistently for all forms of violence in every survey – the challenge is to achieve this. Collecting data on the number of events can be done in one of two ways: by asking for the actual number of events (within a given period, of each form of violence) or by constructing ordinal or nominal categories (such as 'between 1 and 5' or 'too many to count'). The first method should be used, as the second makes it unnecessarily complicated and inaccurate to quantify the number of events. A study using the USA Crime Victimization Survey showed that respondents can consistently report the actual number of events[378]; thus, this is a viable methodology. Collecting data on the number of victims is achieved by counting the number of respondents disclosing or not an experience of each of the different forms of violence. Collecting data on the number of perpetrators is achieved by asking the victim how many perpetrators (and their sex) for each violent event disclosed.

Analysis of the data and its publication should use all three units of measurement.

The process of production of official statistics derived from data reported to the survey has often included the statistical manipulation of the number of events, in a process called 'capping'. Capping is the systematic limitation of the number of repeat events included in estimates of the extent of violence in the population. For example, a respondent may report 20 events of a particular form of violence in the survey period, but only the first five are included. Capping is used to address the issue of volatility when yearly estimates are used to assess trends, because it can adversely affect the reliability of estimates

[378] Planty, M. and Strom, K. (2007) 'Understanding the role of repeat victims in the production of annual US victimization rates', *Journal of Quantitative Criminology*, 23: 179–200.

of change over time. Volatility is a problem when sample sizes are too small to reliably represent rare responses that can differ significantly from year-to-year. However, capping has a significant impact on the accuracy of estimates – both the overall scale and the distribution across different forms of violence. The impact is especially significant for high-frequency repeat victimisation, such as violence by intimate or domestic relations. For example, Walby, Towers and Francis found a 60% increase in the estimated number of violent crimes in the 2011/12 sweep of the CSEW when all reported crimes rather than capped crimes were used. More importantly, they also found that the ratio was not consistent for different forms of violent crime: the estimate of violent crime perpetrated by domestic relations increased by 70% while the estimate of violent crime by strangers only increased by 20%. Volatility in year-to-year estimates can be addressed without the use of capping; for example, by using 'smoothing' methods like three-year rolling averages[379].

Crime and health surveys could be improved. In relation to data collection, they could collect information on the actual number of events, for example, rather than use hard-to-quantify ordinal and nominal categories. They could also consistently collect data on the number of perpetrators for each event. Most importantly, capping should cease. All the events reported to the survey should be included; technical issues of volatility should be dealt with in ways that do not impact on the accuracy of the estimates, such as by aggregating data from surveys in adjacent years to achieve adequate sample sizes.

Violence against women surveys could be improved. Data could be collected on all three units of measurement, including the number of events as well as the number of victims and perpetrators. This is essential in order to take account of the repeat nature of violence by intimate and domestic relations.

[379] Walby, S., Towers, J. and Francis, B. (2014) *Op cit.* Footnote 90. Walby, S., Towers, J. and Francis, B. (2016) *Op cit.* Footnote 6.

Sampling frame

There are three main challenges for the sampling frame: the inclusion of both women and men, preventing the exclusion of those groups most likely to have experienced violence and consistency across countries and over time.

First, the sampling frame should include both women and men so that violence against women and men can be analysed. The causes and consequences of violence against women and men are theorised to be different, but comparative data is needed to test these theories. For example, it has been shown that violent crime against women increased while violent crime against men decreased in England and Wales between 2008/09 and 2013/14[380] . This difference is significant for theory and policy development.

Second, the sampling frame needs to include, not exclude, those most likely to have been victims of violence. Traditionally, survey sampling frames – of both generic crime and health surveys and violence against women surveys – are based on permanent members of residential households. This excludes those temporarily staying with family and friends and those living in group homes or institutions (such as prisons, hostels and other group accommodation), as well as the homeless. These exclusions are particularly important for victims of violence by intimate or domestic relations because many who leave go to stay temporarily with family and friends or go to refuges and are thus excluded by the traditional sampling frame[381]. It is more challenging to include those in residential accommodations and those who are homeless in the sampling frame in ways that are consistent and replicable over time and across countries than it is to include those staying temporarily with family or friends. Jewkes et al.'s survey in South Africa on rape effectively included temporary residents by making the eligibility criteria extend to anyone who had slept in

[380]   Walby, S., Towers, J. and Francis, B. (2016) *Op cit*. Footnote 6.
[381]   Walby, S. and Myhill, A. (2001) *Op cit*. Footnote 355.

the household the previous night[382]. Survey sampling frames should consistently include this latter group.

Third, the sampling frame needs to be consistent across different countries and over time in order to collect comparable data. If different sampling frames are used, the data collected by the different surveys will not be comparable, nor will it be possible to aggregate data over multiple surveys to analyse rarer forms of violence.

Method of survey delivery

There are three issues concerning the method of survey delivery: consistency of approach, high response rates and confidentiality.

First, the same method for delivering the survey needs to be consistently used in order to collect comparable data across different countries and over time. For example, the FRA survey used different methods of survey delivery in different EU Member States, with an initial approach to respondents in Finland, Sweden and Denmark by telephone but with no initial approach by telephone in the other 23 countries. The different survey delivery methods are statistically correlated with the number of women reporting lifetime violence[383]. Thus, cross-national comparisons cannot be reliably made using the FRA survey.

Second, surveys require a consistently high response; the survey delivery method can significantly impact on the response rate. A high response rate is necessary because variations create uncertainty as to the reliability of differences in rates between social groups or countries, especially if the response rate systematically differs between specific groups. For example, the FRA violence against women survey had a low response rate of 42.1% overall, but also had large variations in the response rate in different EU Member States, ranging from 18.5%

---

[382] Jewkes, R., et al., *Op cit.* Footnote 377.
[383] Walby, S., Towers, J. and Francis, B. (2015) *Technical Paper on the Methodology Used by the Paper 'Is violent crime increasing or decreasing?'* www.research. lancs.ac.uk/portal/files/102876063/Technical_Paper_311215_.pdf [November 2016].

in Luxembourg and 19.7% in Sweden to 84% in Hungary. More importantly, the response rate was found to statistically correlate with the number of women reporting violence over their lifetime to the survey[384]. A statistically significant relationship between variations in response rate and reports of violence challenges claims of a 'real' difference between countries.

Third, where the data to be collected is sensitive, as in the case of violence, a high level of confidentiality is needed to give victims the confidence to participate and disclose their experiences of violence. Confidential self-complete methods, such as Computer Assisted Self-Interviewing (CASI), have been demonstrated to elicit higher disclosure rates of violence compared to less confidential methods, such as face-to-face delivery. For example, the CASI-delivered Intimate Violence module of the CSEW elicits a disclosure rate of domestic violence around four times[385] higher than that elicited by the face-to-face Victim Form module for the same sample population. Surveys delivered by telephone have been found to provide lower disclosure rates of violence compared to both face-to-face and self-complete methods[386].

The potential for causing distress by asking respondents to recall potentially traumatic experiences, together with safety considerations for both respondent and interviewer, also need to be addressed in the delivery of surveys. This includes the selection and training of interviewers[387], the provision of information about support services where appropriate and the maintenance of high ethical standards.

[384] Walby, S., Towers, J. and Francis, B. (2015) *Op cit.* Footnote 383.
[385] Walby, S., Towers, J. and Francis, B. (2014) *Op cit.* Footnote 90; Walby, S. and Allen, J. (2004) *Op cit.* Footnote 81
[386] Laaksonen, S. and Heiskanen, M. (2014) 'Comparison of three modes for a crime victimization survey', *Journal of Survey Statistics and Methodology*, 2: 459–83.
[387] WHO (2001) *Putting Women First: Ethical and Safety Recommendations for Research on Domestic Violence against Women*. Geneva, WHO.

5. COLLECTING DATA

Question framing

The way in which questions are framed in surveys has a significant impact on whether or not respondents disclose violence[388]. Questions need to be framed as detailed behavioural descriptions and avoid the use of summary, popular or stigmatised terminology[389]. The terms used for some forms of violence, such as rape, are so stigmatised that respondents will not use them or do not recognise their own experiences in these terms[390]. This has also been demonstrated in relation to the use of terms such as 'violence' and 'victim'[391]. It takes time and space in a survey questionnaire to develop detailed behavioural descriptions; this is an unavoidable necessity for a high-quality survey and should be considered a minimum standard, not 'gold-plating' or an optional extra.

Surveys often use 'screeners' and 'gateways' to guide respondents so they are not asked redundant questions. However, it is important that these do not inappropriately filter out or otherwise obstruct respondents from being able to disclose their experiences of violence. Filters, gateways and screener questions should be kept to a minimum and constructed based on state-of-the-art knowledge of both survey design and the particular form of violence to which they relate.

Violence against women surveys were pioneering in their development of questions using detailed descriptions of behaviour rather than summary, popular or stigmatised terms. This development should continue in relation to further forms of violence and in ways that include information not only on the act but also on the resulting injury or other harm, as well as the intention in the definition of the core concept, in order to achieve comparability with administrative statistics.

Koss, M. (1993) 'Detecting the scope of rape: a review of prevalence research methods', *Journal of Interpersonal Violence*, 8: 198–222.
[389] Walby, S. and Myhill, A. (2001) *Op cit.* Footnote 355.
[390] Koss, M. (1993) *Op cit.* Footnote 388.
[391] Johnson, H. (1996) *Op cit.* Footnote 361.

Adjacent data

Surveys should collect data to assist analysis of the causes and consequences of the violence, in addition to data on the scale and distribution of violence. This should relate to the development of theories of change; for example, how poverty and economic inequality might be related to violence and how service provision for victims might reduce violence.

Way forward: survey data

Sustainable resourcing is an important limiting factor in surveying violence. The cost of standalone specialist surveys is very high; consequently they have rarely been replicated in the way necessary to produce data that is comparable over time. Specialist modules attached to generic surveys are one alternative[392], as in the health surveys in low- and middle-income countries[393]. However, resourcing pressure may make a specialised module vulnerable to being discontinued[394].

The most likely successful new survey model is to embed all the developments discussed earlier − definitions of violence, gender, units of measurement, sampling frame, survey delivery method, and question framing − within wider surveys that are established and receive committed, sustainable resourcing (likely large-scale generic crime or health surveys). This approach is less expensive than setting up a separate survey and less risky than a specialised module. It also has the advantage of mainstreaming the measurement of violence against women and men into the measurement of crime and/or health.

There is a need to coordinate the development of surveys on violence against women and men across countries and over time so

---

[392] van Dijk, J., van Kesteren, J. and Smit, P. (2007) *Criminal Victimisation in International Perspective. Onderzoek en beleid* 257. WODC, den Haag.

[393] DHS. Domestic Violence module questionnaire for women. http://dhsprogram.com/pubs/pdf/DHSQM/DHS7_Module_DomViol_EN_15Jun2015_DHSQM.pdf [November 2016].

[394] Johnson, H. (2015) *Op cit.* Footnote 23.

that the data collected is comparable. This would enable it to be used to reliably populate multiple iterations of indicators in order to analyse progress, as well as to support the further theorisation of the causes and consequences of violence.

The UN should provide guidance and monitoring to ensure national, regional and global surveys on violence meet the aforementioned criteria and the data they collect is comparable, taking account of the quality criteria set forth in this section. This requires coordination between the UN Statistics Commission, the UNODC and UN Women.

Conclusions

The collection and public presentation of data on violence against women and men is currently fragmented, dispersed across a range of agencies and methods, using inconsistent definitions and units of measurement. Yet, sometimes, the raw data collected by administrative authorities and surveys contains such a wide range of information that it would be possible to reorganise it, using the measurement framework proposed here, in order to analyse the data in a coherent and consistent way. The application of a framework that is both consistent and useful for all data users – including services, researchers and policy makers – would not always require substantial new data collection. Rather, it would require applying the framework during the processes of selecting the data that is reported upwards to centralised, national bodies. This requires coordination.

However, in some instances it would be necessary to change the categories within which data is collected – especially to ensure the use of all three units of measurement (events, victims and perpetrators) rather than just the one that local service need prioritises.

Administrative data is usually unsuitable as the basis of an indicator of the rate of violence. This is partly because only a relatively small proportion of victims of violence reports to the authorities. More importantly, it is because of the likely inverse relationship between improving the service and the recorded level of violence. Improving the service is more likely to make the level of recorded violence increase than decrease, even if the improvement in the service puts effective downward pressure on the real rate of violence. The level of violence recorded by an administrative agency (such as the police) is likely to go up if the agency improves their practice, since more people are likely to report to them and the administrative body is more likely to record their report. As such, investing in improvements in practices on – for example – rape is more likely to increase than decrease the recorded level of rape. This means that administrative data, such as that collected via the UNODC ICCS, should not be used as the basis of an indicator. Nor should it be included in any index of equality, such as the EIGE Gender Equality Index.

The usual solution is to turn to surveys, which are more likely not only to record a higher proportion of violence than administrative sources, but also to have a consistent relationship between the level reported to the survey and the level that is 'real'. However, as seen in the previous section, most surveys do not meet the necessary quality standards. They use a definition of violence that is inappropriate (centred on acts and omitting harms and intentions), sample sizes that are too small, sampling frames that are too skewed and methods of approaching respondents that are too diverse to produce reliable and robust results. So, while these have potential, any suggestion to replicate one of the current or past survey instruments should be rejected, even if the budget is limited and continuity appears tempting. Survey methodology has great potential, but it is necessary to insist on quality – otherwise, the skewed data that results will be worse than no data.

There are two exceptions to the rule that administrative data makes for poor indicators. One is where the violence reported to the administrative authorities is close to the real rate – as is the case for homicide. The other is where the indicator concerns not the 'real' rate of violence but the performance of the authorities – as is the case for conviction rates.

Since most people do not report most violence to the authorities, administrative data necessarily only provides partial data on the minority that does; as such, it cannot be used for indicators (again, with the exception is homicide, which usually comes to the attention of the authorities). The best way to identify real changes in the rate of violence, for all forms other than killing, is the survey. Indicators are best populated using survey data – but only if they are of sufficiently high quality not to miss out those who are most likely to suffer violence and only when a new methodology (once established) is then consistently deployed over time and place.

6
COORDINATION

Introduction

Coordination is needed to ensure the development of the coherent measurement framework for violence against women and men, including indicators and the collection of consistent quality data. Coordination includes:

- *Institutions*: to coordinate between countries and international organisations; to monitor, reflect and improve processes, to broker the compromises between agencies that are needed to move towards a single measurement framework and to ensure implementation.
- *Indicators*: to summarise complicated statistics into easy-to-understand figures that benchmark progress.
- *Data collection*: to provide administrative and survey data that reaches recognised quality standards.
- *Data processing*: to process raw data into statistics and agreed indicators.
- *Data linkage*: to ensure it is possible to link data from different sources, while maintaining data protection for individuals.
- *Data protection*: to ensure data concerning individual victims remains under their control and subject to data protection and data privacy entitlements.

- *Publicly available*: to present statistics and indicators to the public, policy makers and researchers in a way that is timely, easy to understand and accessible.
- *Research programmes*: to improve the quality of data collection and utilisation to assist theoretical and policy development.

This chapter discusses policy institutions for planning and monitoring, as well as research programmes. The role of statistical institutions in implementation is discussed in the final chapter.

Policy institutions

In order to move towards the implementation of a coherent and consistent measurement framework, it is necessary to establish mechanisms to secure coordination. Several international and national institutions have a place in this coordination, including the United Nations (UN) (UN Women; UN Office on Drugs and Crime (UNODC); UN Sustainable Development Goals (SDGs)), Council of Europe, European Union (EU) and National Statistical Offices.

Mechanisms through which official coordinating bodies could assist include:

- Providing the context in which agreement on indicators and benchmarks is agreed.
- Providing guidance on the application of agreed definitions to administrative and survey data collection and analysis.
- Providing guidance on the methodology to be used to collect administrative and survey data and its analysis.
- Supporting the development and funding of comprehensive research programmes on violence against women and domestic violence.
- Supporting the mobilisation and coordination of stakeholders (including organisations in civil society), universities (including ad hoc expert groups and networks) and established governmental bodies to develop the quality and harmonisation of data collection and analysis.

- Stimulating debate among a range of publics to develop awareness, provide democratic input and disseminate findings to both targeted and broad audiences.

United Nations

Within the UN, the process of developing cooperation on data collection, analysis and dissemination has involved several activities and entities, including the creation of expert groups comprised variously of academics, NGOs and governmental representatives; the production of guidelines and manuals to facilitate and encourage harmonised methods of data collection and analysis; the establishment and promotion of agreed standards by the UN Statistical Commission and engagement from the Secretary-General of the UN General Assembly, UN Women and regional bodies, such as the UN Economic Commission for Europe (UNECE). While the content is not entirely consistent with the requirements of the *Istanbul Convention*, the range of mechanisms deployed nevertheless constitutes an important set of examples of possible forms of coordination.

Several UN entities have contributed to the coordination of efforts to measure violence and to develop policy to end violence against women. These include: UN Women; the UNODC; UN Statistics Commission; UN Special Rapporteur on Violence against Women; *Convention on the Elimination of Discrimination against Women* (CEDAW), UNECE and World Health Organization (WHO). Several different measurement frameworks have resulted, rather than a single one.

The process of working towards the UN SDGs – which include targeted reduction in violence, especially against women – offers an opportunity to develop coherence within the UN on measuring violence.

Council of Europe

The Council of Europe *Istanbul Convention* identifies the need to coordinate processes of data collection and analysis. Article 1 of the

Convention refers to the need to 'design a comprehensive framework' and to 'effectively co-operate in order to adopt an integrated approach'. Coordination is part of the duties of official bodies that Article 10 requires to be established. Cooperation between these official bodies can assist these developments. Further, the data collected is to be provided to the independent expert body responsible for monitoring the implementation of the *Istanbul Convention* – the Group of Experts on Action against Violence against Women and Domestic Violence (GREVIO[395]) – to assist their work.

According to the *Istanbul Convention*, the data need to be collected on a regular basis (Article 11, paragraphs 1 and 2) – not just once, or on an ad hoc basis. This is because it is important to be able to measure changes over time. In order to measure change, the data needs to be collected in exactly the same categories on a repeated basis; otherwise, it will not be comparable. The Convention does not define how often 'regular' means. Administrative data is often collected on a continuing basis and reported publicly at least annually. This is appropriate for administrative data on violence against women and domestic violence. Survey data also requires regular collection. Some government surveys are annual, which would be appropriate for the forms of violence covered by the Convention. This may be a target to work towards.

It is not enough for the data to be collected and remain inside government agencies or academic archives. It needs to be made 'available to the public' (Article 11.4) so it can inform public debate. To be useful to the public, relevant summaries – such as indicators – should be provided. To be useful to experts, access to databases is necessary. It is also necessary to ensure that, when data is made public, it includes the information relevant to violence against women and domestic violence. It is good practice to bring together this relevant data in a single location that is easily accessible to practitioners, policy makers and the public. A further step is to ensure that the data is comparable between institutions in a country, over time and – ideally – between countries.

---

[395] Established by Article 66 of the *Istanbul Convention*.

Article 65 of the *Istanbul Convention* on Data Protection – which refers to the Council of Europe *Convention for the Protection of Individuals with regard to the Automatic Processing of Personal Data* (ETS No. 108) – states that care needs to be taken not to infringe the privacy of individuals when data is made public. This means, at minimum, ensuring that individuals are not identifiable in data made available to the public. There is also relevant legislation on data protection in the EU, including the 1995 Directive 95/46/EC, Regulation 45/2001 and the 1997 Treaty of Amsterdam[396], which extended legislation to EU bodies. The Treaty of Lisbon established data protection as a legally binding fundamental human right. The 2012 Review of Data Protection has also proposed a draft Directive and Regulation, which is under discussion[397]. It is important to ensure that the holding and transfer of personal data is restricted to protect the victims of violence. Nevertheless, it is also important to ensure anonymised data can be used to inform public policy. This will entail the development of better protocols for sharing data.

The development of data collection and research requires coordination if it is to realise its full potential to support policy development. As well as identifying the need for a national coordinating body (Article 10), the Convention states that information collected under Article 11 is to be provided to GREVIO (Article 66) to assist their work. There are further relevant mechanisms under development to facilitate coordination, including work by UN and EU agencies to develop definitions and internationally comparable classification systems and indicators.

These coordinating bodies should be official government bodies; either freshly mandated existing bodies or newly established bodies. Examples of existing bodies include 'observatories on violence against

---

[396] Europa (2014) *Treaty of Lisbon*. http://ec.europa.eu/archives/lisbon_treaty/index_en.htm [November 2016].

[397] COM/2012/011 proposal for a Regulation on the protection of individuals with regard to the processing of personal data and COM/2012/010 proposal for a Directive on the protection of individuals with regard to the processing of personal data relating to criminal offences. Eur-Lex Procedure 2012/0011/COD. http://eur-lex.europa.eu/procedure/EN/201286 [November 2016].

women', inter-ministerial coordinating structures and expert bodies (such as a research institute or the national statistical institute) that also have a policy mandate. This illustrates the variety of approaches that is possible. These bodies are expressly allowed by the Convention to communicate directly with similar ones in other Parties. They have the ability to 'set up working relations' with counterparts in other Parties in the expectation that this will lead not only to 'important cross-fertilisation that is mutually productive' but also to 'further harmonisation of practice' (*Explanatory Report of the Istanbul Convention*, paragraph 73).

Monitoring by the Council of Europe of the Istanbul Convention

Article 11.3 of the Convention requires that 'the information collected' should be provided to the independent monitoring 'group of experts' established in Article 66 (GREVIO). GREVIO adopted its Rules of Procedure at its first meeting in September 2015, which included their evaluation procedure. GREVIO adopted a questionnaire addressed to national authorities, which included requests for data, in March 2016. The first two national reports submitted by Parties (Austria and Monaco) were received in September 2016 and are available on GREVIO's website[398].

The Council of Europe[399] had already assessed the type of administrative data that Member States were collecting on domestic violence against women. It made recommendations on the collection of administrative data, which levels of state authority and which public or private institutions collect which type of data and how to establish an administrative data system in institutions that do not yet collect the data.

The Council of Europe[400] has been regularly monitoring progress on policy to prevent violence against women in its Member States. Recommendation Rec(2002)5 of the Committee of Ministers on the

[398] Council of Europe (2016) *GREVIO*. www.coe.int/en/web/istanbul-convention/grevio [November 2016].
[399] Council of Europe (2008) *Op cit*. Footnote 313.
[400] Council of Europe (2014) *Op cit*. Footnote 365.

protection of women against violence includes a catalogue of measures to combat the different forms of violence against women: rape and sexual violence; violence within the family or domestic unit; sexual harassment; female genital mutilation (FGM); violence in conflict and post-conflict situations; violence in institutional environments; failure to respect freedom of choice with regard to reproduction (forced abortion or forced sterilisation); killings in the name of so-called honour; and forced and early marriages. Since 2005, the Council of Europe has monitored the extent to which Member States have implemented this Recommendation.

On the basis of voluntary replies from Council of Europe Member States to a standardised questionnaire, progress in the legislative, policy and service response to violence against women has been assessed. The fourth round of monitoring (published in 2014) presented a numerical overview of progress in several areas, including data collection and research on violence against women; it also enables comparison of developments over time and country. It found an overall increase in both the collection of administrative statistics and carrying out prevalence surveys among the general population, although comparability is still low. There are different methods of compiling police data on reported offences by sex and relationship, or reporting on domestic violence. While some Member States are able to extract data and statistics on domestic violence from their general crime statistics, others have established different reporting systems for domestic violence (such as the Netherlands, Poland and Luxembourg). In addition, some research surveys have covered a wide range of forms of violence against women, while others have focused on domestic violence.

European Union

Within the EU, the Commission and its agencies – including Eurostat, the European Institute for Gender Equality (EIGE) and the Fundamental Rights Agency (FRA) – assist the development of cooperation on data collection, analysis and dissemination on violence. There are proposals within the EU – for example, by the Advisory Committee on Equal Opportunities for Women and Men[401] – to develop this capacity further in alignment with the requirements of the *Istanbul Convention*. This includes by adopting an EU strategy on violence against women; establishing an EU Coordinator on violence against women, supported by a network representing national authorities; gathering together in one place information on the implementation by Member States of existing legally binding instruments to monitor progress; collecting standardised and harmonised administrative and survey data; developing standards, indicators, methods and guidelines; providing funding for research on violence against women; and drafting a roadmap on the improvement of data collection on violence against women.

Research programmes

Introduction

Programmes of research are needed in order to not only develop the measurement framework and indicators but also examine the root causes of this violence and thus build the knowledge base for more effective interventions. Research is one of the components of national and international action plans that provide strategic guidance and coordination on the activities needed to reduce and end violence.

The Council of Europe *Istanbul Convention* requires research programmes. Article 11 requires Parties to support research into violence against women in order to study its root causes and effects, incidences and conviction rates. This is essential if the development of policies is to be evidence-based. This research is required to go beyond data collection to studying the causes of the violence, implying contributing to theory construction to explain the connection of causes to violent outcomes. The Convention includes the necessity to study 'the efficacy of the measures taken to implement this convention'. This

---

[401]   Advisory Committee on Equal Opportunities for Women and Men (2014) *Op cit.* Footnote 83.

means there must be monitoring and evaluation of legal and policy developments and an assessment of their efficacy in reducing violence against women and domestic violence. Thus, the Convention requires a well-funded and comprehensive research scheme.

Research programmes can be organised and resourced in a variety of ways and can address a wide variety of topics. They need to support the development of theories of violence in general and gender-based violence against women in particular, which is needed to integrate the implications of empirical evidence into a wider explanatory framework that supports effective intervention. The development of methodology and data collection contributes to research programmes.

Organising and resourcing research programmes

Research on violence against women is organised in different ways: comprehensive and well-funded research programmes, focused research on the implications of legislative developments, research on conviction rates and ad hoc research in universities.

State-funded research programmes to address violence against women and domestic violence as part of a comprehensive strategy are relatively rare. Some states have strategies to support the development and exchange of knowledge that helps to reduce gender-based violence. In these circumstances, research may take place as a component of this wider aim. One example is the EU funding stream originally called 'Daphne', which supports exchange of good practices by supporting projects that sometimes contain a practice-oriented research component[402]. Another example is the research programme concerning specific European countries funded by Norway. There is a programme of research on violence against women in priority developing countries outside Europe, funded by the UK Department

---

[402]   European Commission. *Daphne Toolkit*. http://ec.europa.eu/justice/grants/results/daphne-toolkit/en/daphne-toolkit-%E2%80%93-active-resource-daphne-programme [November 2016]; European Commission. *Daphne III*. www.welcomeurope.com/european-funds/daphne-iii-fight-violence-102+2.html#tab=onglet_details [November 2016].

for International Development. Further, in Denmark, research on gender-based violence has been facilitated by the development of databases containing information about the extent to which victims of gender-based violence use public services. The state has supported the development of 'registers' and relevant laws about data use that make this research feasible. This is not a programme to fund research, but it is a funded activity that facilitates research.

There are funded studies of the implications of specific legislative developments as they come into being. For example, Austria and Germany have both funded extensive impact evaluation research into laws on protection orders to assess their impact and their improvement if needs be. Such impact evaluations of new pieces of legislation are one of the many types of research required under Article 11.

Universities also conduct ad hoc research on violence against women and domestic violence. While there is a thriving community of researchers on violence against women in universities, the field has more usually been undertaken as the result of ad hoc initiatives and the enthusiasm and determination of individual researchers and university-based centres[403] than state-funded programmes. Nevertheless, this is a vibrant field, which includes research addressing the measurement of gender-based violence and would be much enhanced by developing comprehensive and systematic programmes of research.

Reviewing the field

It is important to have regular stocktaking reviews of the developing evidence base in research fields[404]. Such reviews of the state of the art contribute to the development of the field by providing a

---

[403] For example, the Child and Women Abuse Unit (CWASU) at London Metropolitan University

[404] Cullen, F., Wright, J. and Blevins, K. (eds) (2009) *Taking Stock: The Status of Criminological Theory.* New Brunswick, Transaction Publishers.

resource on which other scholars can build[405]. They reduce the likelihood of repetitive researching of the same topics ('reinventing the wheel'). More reviews – repeated on a regular and authoritative basis – are needed. Such reviews should take into account the different methodological practices of different academic disciplines and policy fields. For example, since methodologies that are 'gold standard' in mature, well-developed, long-standing, well-resourced research fields may be currently unattainable in newly emerging fields, care needs to be taken not to exclude relevant knowledge on the basis of inappropriate criteria.

Developing theory

Advancing research depends upon developing theory. The purpose of developing theory is to link empirical observables with underlying causation so as to understand what interventions might lead to prevention. It enables understandings of how the different systems fit together, including their various positive and negative feedback loops and how systems are coupled in the formation of larger systems.

Theory development is always ongoing, building on previous efforts: 'standing on the shoulders of giants'. It is through theorisation that arguments regarding the potential consequences of specific interventions are to be addressed.

One example of a theoretical issue is that of the extent to which gender-based violence is part of a wider system of violence and the extent to which it has its own aetiology.

Developing methodologies and data

Developing research includes developing relevant methodologies and collecting data. The focus in this book has been on quantitative

---

[405] Hester, M. and Westmarland, N. (2005) *Tackling Domestic Violence: Effective Interventions and Approaches.* Home Office Research Study 290. London, Home Office; College of Policing. *What Works: Crime Prevention.* http://whatworks. college.police.uk/Pages/default.aspx [November 2016].

methodologies, since its focus is measurement. However, a full research programme would, of course, entail the full range of scientific methodologies. Qualitative methodologies have their place in this programme, especially in areas in which little research has previously been conducted.

Developing research requires developing systems of data collection, not only data itself. Adequate systems of data collection and analysis will take time and expertise to develop. This needs to be resourced as part of the research programme. The fragmentation of measurement systems within which quantitative data is currently collected is so great that much data is under-used and hard to apply beyond its very narrow frame of reference. A single coherent and consistent measurement system to guide future data collection would significantly assist the development of research in this field.

There is a need to develop the collection of the data required for the measurement framework and its indicators. This includes both the survey to measure domestic violence and the development of administrative data to measure femicide and conviction rates for gender-based violence.

Conclusions

Who is to coordinate and fund these research programmes? There are stakeholders and funders in various branches of national and international governance, as well as entities in civil society – from universities to non-governmental organisations (NGOs) and business. Currently, these are under-mobilised in the support and development of research programmes on gender-based violence.

Most countries have specialised bodies that coordinate the distribution of research funds, such as research funding councils. These typically include both scientifically innovative research and policy-oriented research. Most governments have specialised research programmes tied to assisting government departments' policy development. Within the EU, the specialised body is Directorate-General for Research and Innovation (the programmes of which include both the scientifically-led European Research Council and the policy-oriented Horizon2020 scheme), while many Commission Directorate-Generals (DGs) and their agencies fund smaller policy-related research projects.

There is the further possibility of coalitions of both stakeholders and researchers to co-design future research agendas.

7
A NEW MEASUREMENT
FRAMEWORK AND ITS INDICATORS

Introduction

The purpose of the collection of administrative and survey data and research is to build the knowledge base necessary to combat violence against women and men.

This knowledge base is more effective if benchmarks and summary indicators of changes in violence are sufficiently consistent and coherent to support each other. The use of the same categories to measure the extent and severity of violence in both surveys and the various administrative sources is beneficial for this aim of coherence and complementarity. This is of importance both within a given country and between countries.

The goal should be a single coherent measurement framework for violence against women and men that includes relevant disaggregation. This would provide coherence and enable greater accuracy in the measurement of changes in violence and the effectiveness of public services.

It is recognised that this goal of achieving coherence and alignment of measurement practices is very challenging. The existing multiple measurement practices have developed relatively separately in relation to diverse relevant policy fields and are consequently embedded in disparate frameworks. Some of these policy fields are deeply sedimented in a range of specialised institutions.

The challenge is thus not only mainstreaming gender, but also changing the mainstream so that it embeds those forms of violence that disproportionately affect women. In addition, there is the challenge of ensuring compatibility between diverse policy fields. For example, it is not only an issue of making sure the gendered nature of violence is incorporated in crime statistics, but also making sure that the crime statistics can in some way be made compatible with health statistics.

The process of moving towards greater alignment of these measurement practices – through the implementation of a coherent and consistent measurement framework, so they can better support each other – will require a considerable number of revisions, which can be expected to take some time.

It is necessary to collect administrative and survey data and conduct research to assess and evaluate policy developments that aim to reduce gender-based violence. There are major challenges in meeting these requirements on data. However, there are also some promising practices that are already engaged in the incremental processes necessary to meet these challenges.

Mainstreaming as the way forward

Violence against women and men is relevant to many policy fields, not only the specialised field of violence against women and domestic violence. Ending violence against women and men requires the mobilisation of actors in multiple policy fields, including (but not limited to) the criminal justice system and health services, as well as specialised services for victims. It includes, for example, actors in the employment field (where sexual harassment is an issue), education (which is called upon to promote equality and eliminate gender stereotypes) and media (which have a very important role in challenging or perpetuating attitudes towards violence). It is necessary to cooperate and coordinate multiple services if victims are to have their harms mitigated and efforts at prevention are to be successful. Each of these policy fields currently has a different measurement framework for violence against women and men. It is time to move towards a measurement framework that is relevant to all of these policy fields simultaneously. This process can be conceptualised as 'mainstreaming', drawing on the concept of 'gender mainstreaming'. It develops the concept by applying it not to gender but rather to 'violence'. As in the case of gender mainstreaming, this process involves mutual adjustments in both the 'challenger' perspective (here, violence against women and domestic violence) and the 'mainstream' perspective (including the criminal justice, health and employment systems).

The measurement framework

The measurement framework requires components on violence, on gender and on measurement and counting rules.

Violence

- Actions (and intentions) and harms (and non-consent)
- Variations by types of violence

Gender dimensions

There are five gender dimensions:

- The sex of the victim
- The sex of the perpetrator
- The relationship between perpetrator and victim: whether the perpetrator was a domestic relation – either (current or former) intimate partner of the victim or another family member (either blood relative or other household member), an acquaintance or a stranger
- Whether there was a sexual aspect to the violence as well as physical (potential, not necessary dimension)

- A gender motivation (potential, not necessary dimension)

Unit of measurement

Three units of measurement need to be used at the same time:

- Event (incident, crime, episode and so on)
- Victim
- Perpetrator

For consistency, further issues need to be addressed:

- Ages of perpetrator and victim (adult/minor)
- Temporality (event within the last 12 months; enduring rather than an event)
- Harmonised standards for moment of definition (reporting, investigation, court decision)
- Harmonised counting rules (what takes precedence when there are multiple crimes, victims or perpetrators in the same event)

Indicators

An indicator is a summary statistic that is useful for public and policy makers while being robust[406]. Many proposed 'indicators' of violence have an indeterminate relationship with the 'real' rate of violence. Identifying the relationship between data and the 'real' rate of violence is a challenge. The relationship between the 'statistic', the 'concept' and the 'real world' is not easy to discover. An increase in the amount of violence made visible in administrative or survey data has an uncertain relationship with the 'real' level of violence. There is an ever-present danger that elevating particular pieces of 'data' into 'indicators' of the

---

[406] Berger-Schmitt, R. and B. Jankowitsch (1999) *Systems of Social Indicators and Social Reporting: The State of the Art.* EU Reporting Working Paper No.1. Mannheim, Centre for Survey Research and Methodology.

real rate of violence runs the risk of an inverse relationship between 'recorded violence' and 'real violence'.

Indicators should be relevant for variations in the 'real' rate of different forms of violence and variations in the performance of public bodies, including conviction rates in the criminal justice system.

Three statistics currently meet or nearly meet the criteria for indicators: femicide (gender disaggregated homicide), domestic violent crime and conviction rates for homicide and rape.

Femicide: gender disaggregated homicide

Homicide, disaggregated by the sex of the victim and also by whether the relationship between perpetrator and victim was domestic, is potentially available using administrative data. Counting rules could be provided by the United Nations Office on Drugs and Crime (UNODC) International Classification of Crime for Statistical Purposes (ICCS), with some minor revisions, including elevating the sex of the victim, the sex of the perpetrator and the relationship between them to mandatory codes rather than optional tags.

Challenges to be addressed

There are weaknesses in comparability between countries on counting rules and in the completeness of nationally available data on the relationship between perpetrator and victim.

Domestic violent crime

Violent crime, disaggregated by the sex of the victim and by whether the relationship between perpetrator and victim was domestic (including whether intimate partner or other family member), is potentially available using survey data. Domestic violence is here limited to those types of violence that pass the crime threshold, for practical reasons. The data for this indicator could be gathered by surveys, though currently only the UK (England and Wales) has a survey that collects the relevant information systematically over time.

Challenges to be addressed

Survey methodology would need to meet the standards outlined in the previous chapter, which is currently not the case. Surveys are rarely large enough to reliably capture variations in the rate of other forms of gender-based violence, such as rape. Surveys need to count the acts that are intended to and actually cause harm, as well as victims and perpetrators.

Conviction rates for femicide and rape

Conviction rates for femicide and rape are calculable from available administrative data. These would be indicators of policy performance[407], not of the 'real' rate of violence.

Challenges to be addressed

Some conviction rates for rape in Member States are provided in the European Sourcebook, together with the percentage of rapes reported to the police that are brought to court – but the definitions are not consistent. There has been considerable development in the methodology of conviction rates for rape over the last two decades, tracing the processes through which cases drop out before reaching court[408]. Conviction rates for femicide and intimate partner violence may also be constructed, but will require greater attention to the

[407] Aebi, M. and Linde, A. (2012) *Op cit.* Footnote 193.
[408] Kelly, L. and Lovett, J. (2010) *Different Systems, Similar Outcomes? Tracking Attrition in Reported Rape Cases in Eleven Countries.* London, CWASU; Daly, K. and Bouhours, B. (2010) 'Rape and attrition in the legal process: a comparative analysis of five countries', in Tonry, M. (ed.) *Crime and Justice: An Annual Review of Research.* Volume 39. Chicago, University of Chicago Press: 485–565; Aebi, M. et al. (2014) *Op cit.* Footnote 193; Kelly, L. and Lovett, J. (2010) *Op cit.* Footnote 408.

collection of data in categories that are both identifiable and consistent through the criminal justice system. The construction of comparative conviction rates across the European Union (EU) will require attention to the differences in the processes of prosecution between Member States, including the point at which a case is 'recorded' (when reported or when a decision to prosecute is taken) and the number of potentially intervening stages (including charging and victim withdrawal)[409].

Recommendations to statistical authorities

Introduction

Statistical authorities need to revise their categories for data and indicators in order to align with recent developments in international law, public policy and academic research.

The definitions used by statistical authorities lag behind international law. There have been significant developments in the international legal conventions and the jurisprudence of international courts on matters relevant to gender-based violence, which are not yet incorporated in definitions of violence used by statistical authorities.

Gendered democratic engagement has led to greater political priority to improving public policy to prevent gender-based violence and to assist its victims. The priority given to the ending of violence against women in public policy is not yet reflected in the categories and indicators used by statistical authorities.

The definitions also lag behind developments in academic research. Research has demonstrated the significance of the gender dimension in violent crime and the range of relevant gender-saturated dimensions. This has established the significance of the sex and intimate and domestic relations between perpetrator and victim. Yet, this knowledge is not yet encoded in statistical categories.

---

[409]   Jehle, J. (2012). 'Attrition and conviction rates of sexual offences in Europe: definitions and criminal justice responses', *European Journal on Criminal Policy and Research*, 18: 145–61.

Attention needs to be paid to the statistical categories used in the UN (Sustainable Development Goals (SDGs), UNODC, UN Women, World Health Organization (WHO) and UN Statistical Commission), Europe (Eurostat, European Sourcebook and European Institute for Gender Equality (EIGE)) and the UK (Office for National Statistics (ONS)).

United Nations

Sustainable Development Goals

Reducing and eliminating violence is included in the SDGs, both in general (Goal 16: Targets 16.1 and 16.2) and specifically against women (Goal 5: Targets 5.2 and 5.3). The development of indicators to support these targets should ensure they do not embed different measurement frameworks. This requires the gender disaggregation of the indicators for Goal 16 and the use of the same categories for data in indicators for Targets 5.2, 5.3, 16.1 and 16.2. The UN should implement its policy to mainstream gender, rather than follow the traditional practices of invisibility or gender segregation.

United Nations Office on Drugs and Crime's International Classification of Crime for Statistical Purposes

Measuring violent crime reported to the authorities in a way that is comparable between countries to support policy priorities is the purpose of the UNODC ICCS. The UNODC should recognise the priority the UN accords to its policy to eliminate violence against women by making gender visible in its classification of violent crime and not relegating it to an optional secondary tag.

UN Women

UN Women should implement UN policy on gender mainstreaming and support measurement frameworks for violence against women that embed gender rather than segregate women. This means supporting the development of indicators of violence that are gender disaggregated, rather than those that concern women only.

World Health Organization

The WHO should implement UN policy on gender mainstreaming, make gender dimensions visible in its ICD classification of injuries to health and revise its survey instrument on violence to include men as well as women.

UN Statistics Commission

The UN Statistics Commission should reconsider its indicators on violence against women only and replace them with indicators of violence that make visible all five relevant gender dimensions.

Council of Europe

Group of Experts on Action against Violence against Women and Domestic Violence (GREVIO)

The Council of Europe, in its monitoring of compliance with the *Istanbul Convention* by those Member States that ratify the Convention, should use the measurement framework proposed here. This includes the activities by GREVIO and its associated instruments, such as questionnaires to states.

European Union

Eurostat and the European Commission

The European Commission should regulate Eurostat so that it implements EU policy on gender mainstreaming, which means gender disaggregation and the inclusion of relevant gender dimensions. In relation to violent crime, this means modifying the proposals from the UNODC to collect data using the ICCS so as to elevate to the level of mandatory data collection the five gender dimensions, rather than leaving gender invisible.

European Sourcebook

The European Sourcebook team should revise the categories in which it requests data on violent crime so that they are brought into alignment with UN and EU policy on gender mainstreaming and with international law. This means including the five gender dimensions and revising the definition of rape.

European Commission Gender Equality Unit and the European Institute for Gender Equality (EIGE)

The European Commission Gender Equality Unit should require its agency, the EIGE, to implement EU policy on gender mainstreaming. This means revising the strategy on violence against women only so that instead it becomes one of mainstreaming gender into EU policy and data collection on violence. This means rejecting statistics on women only and replacing them with statistics on violence that are gender disaggregated. In particular, it means rejecting the proposal for a survey on violence that interviews only women and replacing it with mainstreaming the five gender dimensions into EU surveys that include violence.

UK

Office for National Statistics

The ONS should celebrate the quality of the data it collects in the main Victim Form module of the Crime Survey for England and Wales (CSEW) and, in future, publish revised data series that include all the crimes reported to this module. This data should be disaggregated by the range of gender dimensions for which this is possible: sex of victim, sex of perpetrator and relationship between perpetrator and victim. It should acknowledge that, while the higher disclosure rate of the self-completion method in other parts of the CSEW is admirable, it does not compensate for the failure here to collect data on the number of violent crimes.

HM Inspectorate of the Constabulary and UK Statistics Authority

UK police-recorded crime categories should be updated to include the five gender dimensions; or, as a minimum, distinguish between female and male victims for all forms of violent crime, not only homicide and sexual assault.

Ways forward for measurement

Indicators are essential. Building the statistical systems capable of supporting them is challenging.

It is a challenge to develop indicators suitable for all countries. It is appropriate to develop indicators in an incremental manner. The UN needs to offer indicators that are within the capacity of the statistical systems of poor as well as rich countries. In the context of the more developed capacity of the European statistical system, indicators might be possible that have more demanding data requirements than in some other parts of the world. Such a graded approach to developing sophisticated statistical requirements was earlier proposed by the UN

Special Rapporteur for Violence against Women[410]. This started with policy and legislation and moved onwards with simple surveys towards developing more sophisticated survey capacity. Surveys may have started with counting women victims, as in the WHO survey instrument[411], but now need to progress towards a more comprehensive survey instrument that counts events, includes men and has a robust sampling frame.

Developing the theory of change

Ending violence requires a theory of change. Developing a theory of change requires conceptualising and measuring violence. It requires knowing whether violence is increasing or decreasing and if there is more or less in one social location than another.

Developing the theory of change of violence requires the engagement of many sciences: criminology; sociology; women's/gender studies; statistics; social policy; health; law; political science, management and more.

---

[410]   Erturk, Y. (2008) *Report of the Special Rapporteur on Violence against Women.* UN Human Rights Council A/HRC/7/6, 29 January 2008.

[411]   WHO *World Health Surveys.* www.who.int/healthinfo/survey/en [November 2016].

Index

Lightning Source UK Ltd.
Milton Keynes UK
UKHW020104120419
340921UK00022B/924/P

9 781447 332633